Spirit in the P

The journey of a modern medium

By Norman Hutt and Jo Bradley

Table of Contents

Introduction

I first came across Jo Bradley in October 2009, from a link to her website. As a retired scientist, and investigator of mediumship with an open mind, I had been looking for some time in to physical mediumship, within the Noah's Ark Society, and sitting in two physical circles. When I joined Jo's site, I was astounded by what I read on her forum and blog. She had disclosed, and publicised there, many kinds of paranormal phenomena from her private home circle, and also from outside the séance room. This seemed very unusual, and intrigued me. So much so, that I concentrated on finding out as much as I could about Jo's life and mediumship, from her own mouth, in her own recorded words, which provided the data within these pages. I merely edited her words and formed them in to chronological order so that you, the reader, will know what she claims happened, and her interpretation of events.

As a scientist, I used the usual scientific methods to establish facts and the truth of what Jo told me about her experiences, although I had not witnessed them for myself. This included trying to disprove her testimony, by questioning witnesses, and examining any physical evidence, but above all establishing in my own mind whether or not Jo was a reliable, completely honest person whose testimony as to events could be trusted. I found this to be so, after many long conversations and questions, but I still found it very hard to believe, like any rational person. However, the fact that the phenomena took place in lighted conditions, rather than in darkness, which gives rise to doubts about fraud and what is really happening, helped towards drawing conclusions. It doesn't fit with mainstream science at the present time, but I put science above all, and hope that science will one day expand to understand paranormal events as described in this book.

More recently, Jo is attempting to become a full-time medium, branching out in to teaching at physical mediumship workshops and other events, and also developing her other abilities of mental mediumship and healing. I have now been able to take part in workshops, and have witnessed Jo's physical mediumship for myself, which is the only way you can be absolutely sure of the reality. I include some accounts of this next phase of Jo's mediumship, which she hopes and believes will lead to convincing survival evidence. Some of the early physical mediums, like D. D. Home, sat in some form of light, and Jo is working in the old ways of light, but with perhaps a modern slant. Let us **see** what is going on……..

Norman Hutt

"My journey through life has not always been an easy one. Like most folk out there, there have been good times and bad times.

I know that when you start to read of my mystical experiences contained in this book, you will find it hard to believe that such things can occur. Had I not experienced it myself, I would have agreed. Although I have always seen spirit since early childhood, it wasn't until recent years that I became aware of just how much guidance we receive from those living in the spiritual realms, interacting with us in a physical way when necessary.

When you read of such experiences contained within these pages, I ask you to accept the possibility of a psychic force that can be manipulated to interact in our vibration by those who have crossed over. You may well ask, as I did, why? That question is a huge one and brings limitless possibilities, however, my understanding is a simple one, to bring us ultimate proof that no-one dies when their physical body ceases to live, and that love is the strongest emotion one can ever feel.

The experiences described in this book highlight that our physical world is merely a portion of life, like a chapter in an epic book. As my skills have developed and continue to do so, from my interaction with spirit, I feel blessed that I have been chosen to see many chapters of life's book.

Jo Bradley

What is physical mediumship?

Physical mediumship is the production of paranormal physical phenomena. It is the process whereby someone, in Spirit, works or operates through the mental and physical energies of the physical medium and causes something physical to happen on the Earth plane. Physical mediumship is objective in nature; that is, when the phenomena occur, everyone is able to see and/or hear them. It is the rarest form of mediumship, due in part because there are very few people that have the ability to be used by spirit in this way. It is generally believed that only about 1 in every 100,000 people has the correct physical make-up, and it usually takes many years of dedicated sitting to develop, even if the ability is present.

ECTOPLASM: A white, fluidic substance that eminates from the bodily orifices of a medium that is moulded by spirits to assume physical shapes. It manifests as a solidified white mist which has been photographed and has a peculiar smell. It is damaged by exposure to light, which is why seances are held mostly in the dark or dimly lit rooms.

DIRECT VOICE: The voice of a spirit being spoken to the sitters at a séance. The voice usually comes from some point near the medium, but not through the medium. Sometimes a spirit trumpet is used. An ectoplasmic voice box is built by the spirit team which is attached to the mediums vocal chords. The medium is generally in trance, but in rare cases the medium will remain conscious and able to join in with the conversation.

DIRECT WRITING: When spirit's handwriting appears directly on a previously unmarked, unwritten surface.

TRANCE: Trance mediumship or channeling, like so many other forms of spirit communication, is very much misunderstood. In recent years, a number of mediums have called themselves "trance" channels, when, in fact, they were not working in a genuine trance condition. This has been a source of great confusion for many people.
When spirit links with a medium, the spirit communicator exerts various degrees of control, or overshadows the consciousness of the medium to a greater or lesser degree. This varies, depending upon the intent and conditions of communication, as well as the ability of the medium to lend himself or herself to be overshadowed or controlled.
Trance is considered the strongest degree of control. Yet, even here, there are various degrees of trance control: from light trance to very deep trance. Deep trance is used primarily in physical mediumship

LEVITATION: The paranormal raising or suspension of an object or person.

PSYCHIC SURGERY: Psychic surgery is a procedure typically involving the apparent creation of an incision using only the bare hands, the apparent removal of pathological matter, and the seemingly spontaneous healing of the incision.

APPORTS: An apport is the transference of an article from an unknown source, to you, or another place by unknown means. The item can be anything, from coins and jewellery from ancient times, to modern objects such as watches and keys.

Apports are often associated with poltergeist activity, usually out of place items are found around the house and on rare occasions actually being witnessed landing on the floor, in a person's lap or dropping from the ceiling.

Flowers are a well known manifestation at spiritualistic séances. During séances, sitters have also experienced the scent or perfume as it seems to be sprinkled on them.

Conversely, an asport is the transference of a small object from a known location to an unknown location via unknown means.

EVP (Electronic voice phenomena): EVP is the attempt to capture a spirits voice on audio recording tapes. Typically there is no voice heard to the people present in the recording but after reviewing the tapes there are voices recorded.

ETHERIALISATIONS: Etherialisations are comparatively easily produced because they need a lot less power than a full-length cabinet materialisation.

They usually appear to be vaporous and insubstantial - sometimes one can put one's hand right through them - even though they may look solid.

Sometimes they may drape the medium with ectoplasm, and with an ectoplasmic mask superimposed over the medium's features, which can be quite evidential. Usually you are not permitted to touch them.

MATERIALISATION: Ectoplasm is drawn from the physical medium who generally has an abundance of the substance, and a little from each sitter. It is used to mould a physical body of a person in spirit. The materialisations can at first look rather crude, but as the developement continues of the medium, these forms become greater in detail, ultimately forming exact replicas.

TRANSFIGURATION: Ectoplasm is drawn from the medium and a mask, usually placed in front of the mediums face, is formed. Spirit press their impressions of their faces into it so that their earthly features can be seen by all present. Generally a red light is used, but it can be done, depending on the development of the medium, in white light also. No trance is required for this rare form of physical mediumship.

Chapter 1: Early intimations

As a child, Jo had an 'imaginary friend', which her
mother, who was clairvoyant herself, neither
encouraged or discouraged. Jo's child 'friend' stayed
with her until she started school, but then, like many
others born with the gift to connect to Spirit, she
closed down, and made friends in the physical world.
When Jo was about six, Jo's mother was going
through a divorce from her father. Jo had an older
sister, and a younger sister who was only a few
months old. Her younger sister slept in her cot in
Mum's room, and Jo shared the back bedroom with
her older sister.
Her nan's sister was the oldest of thirteen children,
she adored the three sisters, and was married but
childless. She used to come over on the bus every
Saturday, and brought them dot to dot books, so they
adored her too!

During the summer holidays that year, Jo's mum was
quite distressed about her divorce. Jo's aunt invited
her and her older sister to stay with her for about a
week. Her husband,uncle Bert as they knew him, was
in hospital, so it was also company for her. He had
cancer, but Jo and her sister did not know that. They
went on the bus every day, from where the aunt lived,
to Wexham hospital. One day, as they got off the bus,
Jo had this feeling that something was wrong, but
being only six years old, did not know what.
They walked up the driveway of the hospital, and as
they entered the ward a nurse stopped them, and took
their aunt in to a side room. The sisters waited in the

corridor. When she came out she was crying, and said that they needed to get the bus back home. She first made a call from a public telephone box, telling their grandfather to collect them from her house. She didn't tell them that uncle Bert had passed away, only that they couldn't visit him that day.

When they got back to their aunt's home, their granddad was waiting for them, the aunt packed a bag, and got in the car with the girls. Their aunt was taken to Jo's nan's house to stay, and the sisters were dropped off back with mum. Jo and her sister hadn't any experience of death at that time, and mum did not tell them what had happened.
Later in the evening, Jo and her sister went to bed, and after a while, suddenly, a huge 'mass' entered their room. Her sister called across the room, terrified, as she was asking her to get in to bed with her. Jo remembers being very scared, they didn't know what it was,then it got to the bottom of the bed, and it remained still, but was moving within itself. It was like swirling, a grey mass, but did not look human. Jo guessed it would have been as big as a human form. She ran as fast as she could to her sister's bed, they pulled the covers over their heads, and lay there shaking, too terrified to scream out.

The next morning, they told Mum about it, but she said, "Oh don't worry, that was uncle Bert come to say goodbye, he passed away yesterday."
That was Jo's first knowledge of death. She now wonders whether this happened to her because she

was destined to be a physical medium, this being the first signs of materialisation.

Jo felt alone at this time in the physical world, but she was not alone with her spirit friends. Her Mum still speaks about her spirit friend. She said that she used to lay the table for 'Jo's imaginary friend' when Jo was little, for months on end. Jo's spirit friend spoke to her face to face, as natural and normal as to any others, and she always wanted to play what Jo wanted to play, she liked her dresses and toys, everything about her was agreeable. Her name was Jodie. Jo never asked her where she lived. Children accept these things more easily than adults. She left Jo when she went to school. Mum said she was aged six, and her friend had been with her for two years.

Jo attended Sunday school every Sunday. They left her alone and let her draw. Mum went to a school parent evening when Jo was about eight, and spoke to her Religious Education teacher, who said that Jo sat at the back of the classroom, had told her that she was an atheist, and she wouldn't be able to change her mind! Her mum was shocked, but said that Jo went to Sunday school. The teacher replied, "Yes she does, but only because you want her to, you won't be able to change her mind about these matters, she knows what she knows, and it isn't inside a Church!"

Jo had never heard of the Spiritualist belief, or spiritual lifestyle, at the age of eight, but she knew what she saw. She knew there were no dead, just a doorway we walked through, but nobody else seemed to see what she saw.

She had many psychic experiences through her adolescent years. The most predominant was seeing the apparition of her grandfather when she was aged 17. Jo had been absolutely devastated when he had passed on through suffering a heart attack, when she was 16 years old. It took her a long time to come to terms with her loss.

During the years that followed, Jo was busy building a business and raising children, but was reaching a cross roads in her life. The road she chose changed her entire direction. In 2002, whilst on a long weekend in the South of the Country, she had a sitting with a psychic, who had just happened to visit where she was staying. Jo thought it might be a laugh, as the psychic's name was Mystic Mary! Jo was told that she would be going to College to develop a gift that was not being used at the time, she was gathering knowledge for her future work, and had been in training with her life at the time. Jo was sure she was waffling. The word spirit was not used at all, but Jo was said to be an old and wise soul, and that was why the experiences in this lifetime had been so cruel. Jo was sure she was incorrect, as she had never attended College in her teen years, so why on earth would she attend now? But later it did come to pass, with her enrolment at the College of Psychic Studies in London, where what she considers her true journey in her lifetime began to surface.

Two years later, Jo's relationship with her partner was on the rocks. Her mind was fixed on earthly matters, and her children were quite young. She sold her business, and she felt very low. One night, she sat in the dark, all alone with the children in bed, and said out loud, "I believe I know what this is all about." She was searching deep in her soul, for the answers she already knew she possessed. At this point, a light seemed to switch on in her head, and she knew that life is not about money and things, but the people we share our lives with, what we learn from others, who we share our lives with. Jo went to bed praying that she would be shown her true path. She had given no thought to Mystic Mary's reading since it happened.

When Jo woke up in the morning she felt that her room was filled with spirit all around her. She saw them clearly, heard them, and sensed them. From that moment, she started to walk between the two worlds every day. It was like being part of a scene that had been photographed in black and white, and colour, at the same time. The physical scene was the black and white one, and at the same time she saw spirits walking around in beautiful vivid colours, taking no notice of her, like two dimensions in the same space. This happened every day. Then, in February 2004, a strange thing started to happen with her eyes. She had a sensation behind her eyes, and all this energy just flew out of her eyes. It was like a release valve from a steam engine going off. This was weird and strange, and Jo thought she needed help. An advert in a local paper offered telephone readings by a local psychic. Jo called her, and the psychic said, "Ah, you are on a far higher level than me my dear, I cannot connect at your level, you are being waited for at the College."

Jo said College, what College?" " The College of Psychic Studies in London my dear". Jo asked her how she knew that. The psychic said, "I just know!"

Jo decided to contact the College, and they sent her their booklet with all the class details. The courses started in May, 2004, and you had to be interviewed. When the booklet arrived, Jo said to her spirit guides, though she didn't know their names at the time, "Right, highlight the course I need to go in, if I'm supposed to be going to this College." She scanned through the course, and when she got to Tony Stockwell's course, little bright lights appeared, all over it. Jo thought, OK then, she would apply for that one. It was intriguing the way she seemed to be guided in to this course, by Mystic Mary, then the psychic from the advert, then the lights on the booklet, it seemed to her that it was pre-ordained.

On arriving at the College for her first lesson, Jo was ushered into the lecture hall, where there were about 12 students in all age ranges. They were a lovely friendly bunch, and after introducing themselves to each other, they sat waiting patiently for their tutor to arrive. When Tony came into the room a few moments later, he called a warm hello to everyone, then said, "Um this is strange, we dont usually sit in the lecture hall to teach classes." It was at a later date that Tony found out a reason for being issued with the hall.
A couple of weeks later after starting College, a strange thing started to happen during meditation. In the lecture hall at College, there hung a portrait of a

man. Jo had no idea who he was at that point, all she knew was that during meditation she felt that the man in the portrait kept coming to her. She thought it was her imagination, until during her next visit to College, she was standing in front of the picture, gazing up at the man in the portrait and deep in thought, when she heard Tony say, " Who is he Jo? " Jo replied, " I have no idea".

Later in class, Tony gave an exercise for the students to do and left the classroom for a few minutes. He smiled at Jo when he returned, and as the class finished he asked to have a word with her.
He said that the man in the picture was Daniel D. Home, that he had been a physical medium during his time, and that Daniel had spoken to him during class. Daniel had said that he was an ancestor of Jo, gave his age at his passing, and other personal details which all turned out to be correct. Tony said that Jo was born with the gift of physical mediumship also, and that when she started to levitate too......She looked at Tony, she thought the man had gone mad. Physical mediumship, whats that? Levitation, yeah right! She came home on the train that night, her mind whirling, not really knowing what on earth it all meant. She surfed the web to find out what she could about physical mediumship, and her jaw dropped open when she read accounts of mediums such as D.D. Home, Helen Duncan and Minnie Harrison.

During Jo's time at the College, she was asked by a woman at the local Spiritualist Church if she could have a reading. Jo used to do about a dozen a week back then, so she agreed. The woman came round, it was a sunny day, the sun was streaming in through the lounge windows, so Jo pulled the curtains for comfort, but it wasn't dark at all. They sat on sofas facing each other. A gentleman wearing a uniform stepped forward from the Spirit world for the sitter, and he started highlighting his boots. Jo can't remember why now, but it helped to identify him in some way to the sitter.

All of a sudden these boots materialised, and started walking across the room!

Jo leant forward, mesmerised by it! The sitter screamed, and ran out of the house.

The boots instantly sank to the ground as she left, and were gone.They both saw the boots objectively, so it could not be described as imagination. Jo never saw that sitter again at the Church, after that experience. She thought it was a fascinating event, but she did not have a clue how it happened. This was clearly objective paranormal activity, as they had both seen the same event, not explainable by normal means.

Jo also used to give light trance healing in her séance room. The sitters would listen to direct voice, mostly their names being called. On one occasion, a sitter jumped, and it gave Jo a slight jerk, so she had to warn people. On another occasion, Jo was sat in her living room with the former editor of Psychic News, when a light suddenly appeared on the floor between them.

Jo decided to start holding physical seances, to see if anything would happen. There seemed to have been so many pointers towards this spiritual pathway, but she had no idea what would happen. She gathered a small bunch of her friends, and they sat nervously round a small table in a blacked out room, with one candle alight in the centre of the table. Objects started to move, taps were heard at differing points in the room, and a black mass appeared on the table before them, which within a few seconds formed the shape of a hand which glided across the table before melting away. Jo's friend was horrified, as it was going in her direction, she squealed, and it sunk into the table. They ended the sitting to discuss what on earth had just happened.

They sat on the sofas, still with candle alight on the table, and the same friend who had squealed started to giggle uncontrollably, her head fell forward, and when her head was raised again, her eyes had gone black. Jo called her name, but she did not respond as herself. Jo was completely intrigued by the proceedings, and her other friends were quite nervous, however the friend started to say, "You don't know, you don't know." Jo said, "What don't I know?" The friend's voice said:

"They put you (Jo) in a trance just as you are drifting off to sleep and levitate you, when they take you out of trance and back down you are still asleep. In 6 days time (it actually turned out to be146 days later) your new guide will be with you completing the triangle, you will know when this has happened, your furniture will be re-arranged, you have to learn about your new guide, and the new energy that will surround you."

Thinking back, Jo didn't know why all this did not

terrify her, but it didn't, it fascinated her. Jo had no previous experience with circle sittings, and this was not in a blacked out room, it was in the lounge with the curtains drawn and door shut, but not total blackout like you get in dark seance rooms. She was experimenting because of what Tony had said to her about physical mediumship, just to see if anything would occur. They only sat the once together, Jo thought the others were too nervous after that event to do it again!

Jo thinks that her friend spoke in trance, although at the time she would have been unable to clarify it, as she had no experience of trance other than witnessing Tony on one occasion. It was a one-off for her friend, but Jo thinks that her guide Dan needed to speak with her, and seized his opportunity, but it happened to her daughter once also, with the poltergeist event. She has never tranced since, although Jo knows that her daughter could be a really good medium if she chose to work with spirit. The friend has never been a member of Jo's circle, neither has her daughter.
Jo had guides but she didn't then know their names, other than Dan, who Tony had identified. Jo's friend was not a church goer, and as far as Jo knew had only the usual religious education at school. She had lost two babies, and found comfort in the spiritualist community at the Spiritualist Church, where Jo met her.

Back at College, Tony encouraged Jo to start a physical circle, telling her to search on the web for as much information as possible first, so that she would be well equipped with much knowledge. There is little help on the web, apart from the wonderful accounts of past mediums, and the evidence brought by their mediumship. Incidentally, the lecture hall at the College was the only room in which Daniel's portrait hung, so Jo thought that he might have had a hand in guiding her to him. As for him being an ancestor of her's, Jo began a long term tracing of her ancestry, in order to find out if there was any truth in that statement.

Jo had started in the mental mediumship foundation class, where she met Micky , who became a close friend and fellow medium, and stayed in that class for one term. Tony then moved her to the advanced class, but told her after one term that he couldn't teach her anything further, but he was running a short course on physical mediumship, and she needed to be there. So Jo went to it. She started to understand the sensitivity better. Tony said that he knew the first time they did a meditation session that Jo was a physical medium. Jo asked him how he knew, and he said she had full transfiguration, he couldn't take his eyes of her, she had gone completely! Jo said, "Oh, what's transfiguration?" This was all completely new to her.

Tony then asked Jo to attend a trance healing workshop, because by that time she had channelled psychic surgery. Jo arrived late for this, because the trains were running late. When she finally arrived, all heads turned and stared at her as she entered the room. Tony simply smiled, and said," Ladies and gentlemen, this is the lady I have been telling you about." Jo didn't know where to put herself, wondering what on earth he'd been saying! Tony barred Jo that day from allowing psychic surgery, although he really wanted to see it himself. The College didn't have the right insurance to cover the class. Jo had no idea how to control psychic surgery, it just happened! Tony Stockwell is a very gifted medium, and it was in part due to Tony's encouragement, and his acknowledgement of physical phenomena, that Jo began to sit for development as a physical medium.

Jo decided to start holding further experimental physical seances, to see if anything would happen. On 25th August 2004, Jo's guide 'William' produced his solid hand and placed it on a luminous plaque on the table, it appeared black, but his hand was enormous, far larger than any male's hand Jo had seen before. It was perfectly formed in every detail, including his fingernails, which he repeatedly tapped to show the strength of it's solidity. This was witnessed by all three in the circle.

Jo left the College in the December of 2004, and continued to hold seances at her home. Furniture continued to move about, apports started to drop from the ceilings, crystals dropped in, notes with writing on them appeared.

Occasionally, voices would be heard from a space in mid-air. Jo felt that the time had come when she should really start a circle, and sit for the development of this potentially wonderful healing form of mediumship. She placed an advert for sitters, and the group ' The Circle of Friends' was formed.

Jo thought there was a reason why such strong phenomena had happened, when she had only just started sitting as an experiment. She still doubted back then, although she knew what Tony had said to her, and he had directed her to read up about people like Helen Duncan. She had not witnessed for herself yet, and she thought that the only way for her to truly believe and understand her mission was for the spirit team to bring her ultimate proof. She was working towards full form materialisation in the light, but she recognised there is a vast difference in development between full form and showing a hand or a foot. She often thought whether or not she would have decided to sit and develop with such dedication, if the proof Tony had told her about had not taken place. Maybe she wouldn't have. Those first materialised hands gave her encouragement, a proof that these things were indeed possible

<u>Chapter 2: The Circle of Friends</u>

In January 2005, the Circle of Friends sat for the first
time. The circle had seven members: Jo sitting in a
make-shift cabinet, her ex- partner, who was a very
good friend, two neighbours also friends of hers, a
friend from the local Spiritualist Church, and two
men who had responded to an advert she had placed
looking for sitters. None of them had ever sat in a
circle before, so they were all committed to learning
together.

The group met for the first time on the 7th January.
The sitting was held in Jo's lounge with the windows
and door completely blackened out. There was a
cabinet made from old poles and covered in black
material, with an ordinary dining chair inside, for Jo
to sit on.Taped music was played on the stereo. Just
outside the cabinet was a card table, with a little
luminous paint on each corner of the table, so that the
sitters had some source to see if the table moved at
all. A candle was alight. A sitter had been given
permission to take random photos with his digital
camera,in the dark, and with the flash disabled. The
sitting began at 8pm, after they had ensured that all
mobiles in the house were turned off, the phone had
been disconnected, and that no sitter had loose
change, keys or any other objects that could disturb
the sitting. Jo entered the cabinet and made herself
comfortable on the chair, whilst the others sat on the
sofas, forming a circle.
A prayer was said, and the music played. Singing was
done to heighten the vibrations.

Jo sat inside the cabinet not really knowing what she should do, and wondering if the proceedings had been carried out correctly.

Suddenly, she heard the sitters exclaim in very surprised voices, " Look at the table, it's in the air!" Jo wanted to poke her head out of the cabinet as she was so surprised, but managed to resist the urge. The sitter with the camera said, " I'm going to take a few random snaps to see if anything can be caught." Jo kept asking for updates, and each time was told the table was still floating in the air, which was quite remarkable.

Jo settled herself back down, and a few moments later, she felt what can only be described as something swirling around her entire body, but it started at her feet, and the air became icy cold inside the cabinet. Moments later she was aware of the sitters talking about something white that they could see floating out of the cabinet. The camera was aimed at it, and a picture snapped. The 'sensation' disappeared from inside the cabinet, and as Jo was trying to relay what had happened to the sitters, the table floated back to the ground. The energy dropped, and the circle was brought to a close, with them giving thanks to the guides, and a short closing prayer.

As they left the lounge and headed for the dining room for refreshments, they were all chatting excitedly about the evening's events. They switched on the computer, uploaded the pictures from the camera, and were startled with the result of the picture taken of the white object floating from the cabinet. Jo thought it was of a man, complete with beard, floating on his side, very remarkable.They were stunned to see this. It was on seeing this image, that it was decided they should keep any evidence between the circle members.

Unfortunately, the owner of the camera took away the digital evidence in the camera, and the PC image was lost, due to the computer breaking down. The witnesses remain, however, to testify what happened. Much later, the photo was fortunately retrieved, to add to the physical evidence from the seances.

Also in January 2005, Jo started to receive hand written apported notes, which gave the names of who were thought to be guides, and spoke of levitation and the circle work. They all arrived in broad daylight over a two day period, and seem to be unique for three reasons:

(a) they werc apported

(b) produced through direct writing

(c) gave answers to questions that Jo asked throughout that two day period.

The paper they were produced on did not come from her home. They were warm to the touch moments after arriving. Along with the notes, other apported objects were received.

On 17th January, a friend called around to Jo's home in the evening. She was a member of the circle, but she had come to meditate with Jo. They relaxed, chatting happily with a cup of coffee. It was a very cold night in the middle of January. A little while later they decided to meditate. Jo's daughter, aged 14 at the time, was at home, and her son was in bed. The daughter asked if she could remain in the room while they meditated, assuring them that she would sit very quietly and not disturb them. Jo trusted her completely, so agreed, and she and her friend sat on one sofa, while her daughter sat on the other. They had been meditating for about 20 minutes, and Jo remembers starting to come back from a wonderful place, when all of a sudden she heard a sudden noise in the room, and her daughter let out a little squeal.

Jo quickly grounded herself, before opening her eyes and looking at her. Jo's friend was also looking at her, somewhat strangely. Jo was about to ask her why she had squealed and ask what the noise had been, when suddenly the sofa she was sitting on shot about a foot to the left.

She stared at it, wondering what was going on, then the sofa she was sitting on started to vibrate, and shot a couple of feet to the right. They were all very bemused by this. The sofas continued to shift from left to right, for about ten more minutes. Jo's elder daughter, who had gone out for the evening, then returned home. They were laughing excitedly to themselves when she entered the room. She asked why they were laughing, as she slumped on the sofa next to her sister.

Jo smiled and said, "No reason". No sooner had Jo replied to her, than she said, "And why is this sofa vibrating?". She barely got to the end of words, when the sofa shifted again to the right. " What the ..." The daughter was surprised and rather shocked. Around 11pm, things seemed to have quietened down, so Jo's friend went home and the family retired to bed.

The following morning, Jo's eldest daughter had an appointment, so was the first to rise. Jo heard her go downstairs, and within a few seconds she called up the stairs to her and said, "Mum, why have you put the sofas in the middle of the living room"?
Jo hadn't done so, because they had all retired to bed the previous night at the same time. It looked like whoever had made their presence known to them the night before had decided to re-arrange the furniture whilst they slept!
Jo decided to get up and go downstairs. She wrapped herself up in a snuggly dressing gown, put the sofas back, and went and put the kettle on. Her younger daughter came down, switched the TV on, grabbed a throw as the morning was a frosty one again, and wrapped herself up cosy on the sofa. Jo made the tea and settled down to watch a morning movie with her, whilst her other daughter headed for her appointment.
The film finished about 11am, and Jo announced to her youngest that she ought to go get washed and dressed, as she had some shopping to do. She headed upstairs to her bedroom, to get some clean clothes, before having a soak in the tub. As she entered her bedroom, there laying on her bed were three sea shells which had been taken from her bedside cabinet, and had been placed in the shape of a triangle. Jo stood there pondering on this sight for a few moments, before yelling downstairs to enquire if her daughter had been in her room. The answer was no. Jo asked her to come up and take a look at the shells,

which she did , and immediately said, "Why have you done that , mum?" Jo replied that it wasn't her. They were still pondering on it when they left her bedroom.

They started to head back downstairs as Jo headed for the bathroom, when they heard a bang from Jo's room. They looked at each other, said nothing, and headed back together to Jo's room. This time, on the bed above the shells, Jo's books, which had been stacked in a pile on the cabinet, had been placed above the shells like a rainbow. They were understanably quite bewildered by this.
Jo went for her bath, dressed, and went back downstairs, to encourage her daughter to bath and get ready to go shopping. She was grumbling about having to go out in the cold as she disappeared upstairs to her room. Moments later Jo heard her calling to her, "Mum....you'd better get up here." Jo went up to see what the problem was.
 Her daughter said, " What have you done with my duvet?" Jo said she had not been in her daughter's room, it was where she left it, she supposed. "Well, it was on my bed, and it's not there now."
They found it on the top of her wardrobe of all places, not put there by them. However, with the problem solved, Jo went back downstairs to get a few chores done while waiting for her daughter. As she entered the living room, the sofas were back in the middle of the room. Jo just laughed, someone was determined to re-arrange the house that day!

Her elder daughter arrived back home from her

appointment, was bursting for the loo, and ran upstairs to the bathroom. Jo heard her say, " What the....!" A couple of minutes later she came back down, and said, "Why have you put your candles in the bath in the shape of a triangle?" Jo said she hadn't, the house was being re-arranged by 'someone' who obviously liked triangles! Jo did the washing up, left it draining, gathered her daughters, and headed for the supermarket, pondering about who on earth was doing all of this within their home.

They arrived back about an hour later, and as they walked back in through the front door, boy, what a mess they found. It looked like they had had a party and not tidied up. Cushions had been scattered off the sofas, candles around the house were placed in to triangles, and when Jo went to the kitchen to put the shopping away, she was greeted with the washing up that she had left draining stacked high, balanced on each other, on the kitchen work top. She was mystified, as they stood there and asked, "Who is doing this?"

Jo got her answer within minutes. As she went back through to the dining room, to get the shopping bags, she heard a loud thud from above her head. It came from her bedroom She called to her youngest daughter, and asked her to go investigate. A moment later she called, "Mum, mum, there is a note on your bed !" Jo went to see, and true enough, laying on her bed in the centre of a triangle made from the shells, was a handwritten note. The names, Helen, Dan and Will had been written on a small piece of paper that had obviously been taken from a small note book, but not from their house. The note was warm to the touch. Jo stared at it in sheer amazement. It appeared that it was Helen, Dan and Will doing all this!

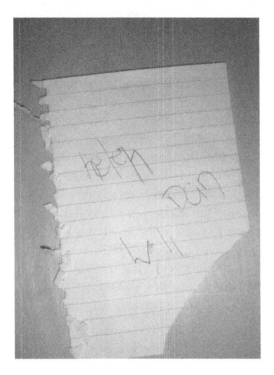

She proceeded to ask questions all day long, the notes continued to come in answer to her questions, all written on the same paper, and to this day, she has never found out where 'they' took it from. In the end, 23 notes were left by 'them', and all were stored for safe keeping.

The activity continued all the following day too, more apports were literally dropping from the ceiling. These apports were varied items, were materialising during daylight, and literally falling from a space above her head. Crystals, flowers, rose petals etc, the house became even busier as friends started to call around to see this wonderful phenomena, and they were not disappointed.

Jo explains what her feelings about it were like at the time:
" Well that was mind-blowing, materialising in mid-space above my head from nowhere, I mean, that was just truly amazing, and mystifying at the same time. I always used to say, wow, how do you do that? It was amazement mostly though, never fear in my mind. It made some fearful I guess. It was not only me, but family and sitters and friends who witnessed it. They tried to explain it away, mostly with 'What the …..!' , a natural reaction I guess for most people. Normally followed by 'You're weird, you are!' I had no answers to offer them, just things for them to witness. They couldn't dispute the evidence of their own eyes, could they? I have no idea what thoughts went through other people's heads. I was in awe of what they did around us. Well, you're sitting at the dining room table, doing your makeup to go out for the evening, and your daughter is sat opposite also doing her makeup, and nobody else is at home. From above me, tiny green beads fell and scattered all over the table. There really is no explanation other than the paranormal to be found. And that's what it was like. Shelley just looked up, then looked at me, and said something like 'Oh they're pretty, thank you!' It became an accepted part of ordinary life. That sounds blasé I know. Of course it's hard to believe if you haven't seen it for yourself, but it's nonetheless the

truth. I don't expect readers of the book to believe at all, but I do hope that some might feel inspired to investigate the subject further. Or if there is someone else out there, experiencing similar phenomena, to know that it is normal, it does happen to others, and hopefully bring them comfort in knowing they aren't going mad. Maybe even inspire them to sit and develop their own gift. I think the person who probably had the hardest job at accepting the paranormal events was my circle leader,Terry. He had been raised by an Irish staunch Catholic father. Jason has witnessed most things too, like direct voice, and materialised hands. Alec gives a report of what he experienced."

Chapter 3: The strange case of Lucy

Also in January 2005, Jo decided to buy an ordinary tape recorder, to try out electronic voice phenomena (EVP.) That evening she went to bed, and while reading, decided to put the tape recorder to record, in the unlikely event of picking up some EVP. The room was quiet, accept for the occasional turning of the page. After about 20 mins, she decided that it really was time for sleep, she rewound the tape, pressed the play button, switched off the lamp, and laid back listening for any noises. About 10 minutes s into it, a lady's voice, very clearly and very distinctly, was heard saying, " It's Lucy". Jo almost leapt out of bed, she was so amazed that a voice had appeared on her first attempt.

In February 2005, Jo awoke in the night, her heart racing, believing that she had had a nightmare. She had been in a room, in a very old building, with low ceilings and crooked windows. She was facing the door that led into this bedroom. She saw two steps down on entering the room, and there was a window to her left. As she looked out of the door, she could see a straight landing leading to other rooms. The bed, which was on the far wall, was covered in a flowery bed spread. She knew this room was over an old working room, like a pub from hundreds of years ago, or some sort of shop. As she stood looking at the door out from the bedroom, a dark feeling came over her, and she sensed spirits filing down the corridor and into the room. As they entered they started forming a semi-circle around her, moving closer and closer in towards her. It was at this point that she awoke.

The following month, on March 14th 2005, Jo's daughter Natalie, who was 14 at the time, came home from an evening out with friends. Jo was sitting on one sofa watching TV, and Natalie said hello as she came in. She told Jo about her evening for a few minutes, and then she sat on the other sofa. Jo continued to watch TV, and after about 10 minutes she noticed that her daughter had nodded off to sleep. Jo called to her to go to bed, but there was no response. Jo called to her again to go to bed, but as she glanced in her direction, her daughter's head slowly rose, and she turned towards Jo. Her eyes had become very dark, then a voice suddenly said, "Natalie is not here". Jo was quite stunned, but responded, " Oh I'm so sorry, who am I speaking with?" Natalie replied, "Lucy".........the same name as on the EVP tape from January! 'Lucy' asked Jo for pen and paper, which she duly got, and handed them to her. She took the pen in her left hand, although Natalie is right handed. Without taking her eyes away from Jo, she drew a picture of a house, and also drew an arrow pointing at the house with '7 spirits' and various other things.
Natalie was still gazing at Jo, and the entity claiming to be Lucy said, " A man will be brought to you, you must help him". Jo said OK, but when?
 Lucy said , " Four months, exactly four months time," and with that Natalie's head gently dropped forward. After a few minutes she stretched, as if coming out of a sleep. Natalie had no memory or

knowledge of this event afterwards. Jo wrote the date on the back of the picture, and placed it in a folder for safe keeping.

On July 1st 2005, a friend rang Jo, and asked if she would see a friend of his, who had a chronic back complaint. She agreed. A couple of days later that friend called her to make an appointment, and it was agreed for him to come on July 7th. As it turned out, this appointment was cancelled, due to the bombings in London, so it was re-arranged for the following week, the 14th. He arrived at the time specified, and after a healing session, Jo asked if he would like a cup of coffee before leaving for home, which was in Folkstone. As they sat chatting over a coffee, he said something, Jo can't remember what exactly, but she went to the folder and pulled out the drawing of the house. He went white and immediately asked where she had got the drawing from, as it was his house, in every detail ! Jo was as gobsmacked as him, but on looking at the date on the back of the drawing, discovered it was exactly 4 months ago. Jo described his bedroom in every detail. The poor man just sat there, his mouth wide open. She asked him what was beneath the bedroom, he said his lounge, but that back in the 1400's it had been the village bakery. She then told him that she thought he had really bad poltergeist activity in his home, and explained the strange message of him being brought to her. He sighed, and said yes, that not even his family would go into his home, as voices were heard shouting at them to get out, and doors would slam in their faces when they tried to enter certain rooms. It was agreed

Jo would visit the following week.

Jo made the long trip to Folkstone on July 21st, a journey well over 100 miles from where she lived. Three members of Jo's circle travelled with her to Folkestone.
She didnt have a clue why this man had been brought to her, and had never dealt with this kind of problem before. She was extremely nervous about facing it, without any experience. But like always, she trusted her guides completely, and was confident they would be in control of the situation. As they entered the house, it had a horrid heavy atmosphere, almost like a smog, which engulfed the house. Jo went from room to room downstairs, but could feel spirits all around her, staring at her defiantly. She did manage to hold her nerve. As they went upstairs, a bedroom door slammed, cutting her off from the rest of the group. She closed her eyes, and prayed like she had never prayed before. Eventually, the door opened, and she moved to the next room, where the majority of the activity was happening.

They joined hands and started praying again, asking for the entities to leave the house and it's owners in peace. Lights were flashing on and off in the room. It was a scary moment, and something that Jo hopes she does not have to face too often. The house is peaceful now, and the atmosphere completely changed, it is warm and bright now. The owners still call Jo occasionally, to just report that all is still quiet.

<u>Chapter 4: Circle build-up</u>

On 20th April 2005, five voices were heard from seperate places in the seance room. And then on 22nd April 2005, a strange energy was felt around the sitters feet, the floor started to vibrate, and a woman was heard singing in the cabinet. Not the medium! During the séance on 27th April 2005, a trumpet lifted and swung back and forth, and a blowing sound was heard, coming through the trumpet at the sametime.

There was more trumpet movement on the 29th April séance. On the 4th May 2005, light was brought into the seance room by the spirit team, and there was more trumpet movement. Again there was more trumpet movement on the 6th May.

During the 11th May séance, there was floor vibration, and once again there was trumpet movement. On the 25th May 2005, physical touches were felt, cold breezes, and raps and taps heard on the table and walls. On the 15th June 2005, a bee was heard buzzing in the seance room, although on checking after the sitting, no bee was found in the room. Voices were heard whispering, and bangs and raps heard.

On the 20th June 2005 (Jo's birthday), the Zerdin Fellowship made contact with the group. On 1st July 2005, a representative came from the Zerdin Fellowship, to sit in their home circle. He had a lot of knowledge of physical mediumship, and advised the group on safety issues and correct procedures , and continued to come for about four more weeks. They learned a lot from him, for which they were grateful, but the group decided not to attach themselves to any organisations, and to remain completely an independent group. It was also on this evening's sitting that Jo received a burn across her eyebrow which blistered, from the curtain being pulled back from the cabinet, before all the ectoplasm had retracted back, so caution is obviously necessary for the medium's safety.

On 27th July 2005, a new sitter was interviewed for the group, following the departure of one of the original group, then on 5th August 2005, the new sitter felt a solid hand grab her thigh. She was very emotional about this. On the 12th August a faint "hello" was heard by two sitters in the circle. A grumbling was heard in circle on the 25th August, and some table movement without a physical touch aiding it. A man announced " I am here" on the 2nd September, a solid leg was felt by a sitter, and there was stomping on the floor. During the 9th September 2005 séance, a partial manifestation was seen floating out of the cabinet, and on 25th September a finger manifested and was felt by a guest sitter.

Jo decided to have a trance reading with Jay Love, at the College of Psychic Studies, on 13th March 2006. She was given information from the medium's guide about her development and personal life. Jo was unknown to the trance medium before the sitting. She was told that she was a very strong individual, and had overcome great difficulties. She had great links with Spirit, her attunement. Her mind was very vast, and Spirit formulates before her eyes. Phenomena occurs sporadically, and she had the potential to bring out this form of mediumship. She possessed knowledge to produce physical mediumship.A decline in health, not enjoying certain foodstuffs, which is preparation from Spirit. Jo was likened to John the Baptist, everyone has an aspect of a Saint attached to them. She has a higher mind, an understanding of trance. The Group were brought together for a reason. There is a great 'quickening' with the circle, and they are standing aside practising, before bringing in to the room. Gordon Higginson was working behind the scenes, and Jo had the capabilities to manifest great things.

Jo was advised to be careful about attaching to an organisation. Sanctions would be imposed, and she should remain free. She will give great knowledge to many people.

Spirit were pleased she was bringing back what was needed to be brought back.

She should not allow any individual to put their ideas upon her, it is her choice, not their's. Jo was very gifted, but had suffered very traumatic times, which had hardened her greatly. There were more hard times to come, but she should always follow what is right for her. Her words will be in a book. She has a very analytical mind, and gives truth to others. Jo was linked to people in the spiritual movement, important people that were high up in the spiritual movement. She was a very learned soul, her mother was very mediumistic, and it was wonderful passing it on to her children. Jo is a teacher, with very good quality energy. Some people entered her life to take her energy. They want her to work with Spirit, not behind the scenes. They want a change if diet, exclude meat or dairy. Her guides were changing, just a few, 'Auriel' very positive.

Within one year, Spirit will manifest. If there is any hostility, remove the individual from the circle. Direct voice, use of energy sporadically, depending on the physical body, many phases. Within six months, there will be more voices, continue in the dark for the current time. Interference with a woman's natural cycle, do not worry.

Jo thought this reading was very encouraging for her future in physical mediumship, following Tony Stockwell's help and advice, and the physical phenomena already experienced.

Chapter 5: First Paul Case trance reading

A friend of Jo then recommended a terrific trance medium, named Paul Case. Her recent sitting with him had been bang on the mark, she said, and she had been very impressed. Jo did not feel that she really needed to sit with him, but had a sense of curiosity. She wanted to know if his guide would pick up on all the physical phenomena, which she and others had experienced. Jo phoned to make the booking, and Paul's partner answered. He simply asked for her Christian name, and no other details whatsoever. Jo gave it as 'Joanne', her full Christian name. She was known to every body as Jo, and a possible connection with her and physical mediumship could have been made, to anyone who knew her history, if she had given that name.

 Jo and her circle leader were thus unknown to Paul Case, the trance medium, and they could have been anybody coming in off the street, with any kind of spiritual gifts, or with none. The taped recording of the reading was transcribed and is as follows:

"I come. My name is Red Cloud. It is my honour to be here. As I link with the energies there is a circle of many minds in the Spirit World who watch you with great interest. There has been much emotional pain and turmoil that has brought you in to this place. A place of healing, understanding and peace, but it is not without complications for there are always those who seek to control, for their own purposes.
And it is with great excitement I can see you have moved through this learning, and you have found

yourselves on the shores of a pleasant land, a land where you will grow with much sunshine in your hearts, for you, as with many, are impatient, and you feel that you have not progressed, you feel that you have lost your ability to sense the presence of your guides and helpers. But let me say to you, that you are merely moving through frequencies of light, in to a frequency of greater clarity, where you will set aside your doubts of yourself, and you will move in to a knowing place, a place of confidence, where you will not be perturbed by the criticism of others, who seek from their stance of jealousy to undermine your confidence, you understand.
It is in this place that you will be joined by others from our side of life.

For it is I am told there is a team of science, knowledge, that comes, that they wish to bring tangible evidence from the world of Spirit, in to the physical plane, that you may see with your physical eyes, and there will be ramifications with works of healing also, for there will be, as time goes on with your work, the need to manifest this energy in a healing way, and you will be given guidance for the voice will come with you, voice will come, for both of you are linked with this work, both in different ways, but you see voice will come to both, but you will share the burden of giving of your energy whilst one develops, another will give, whilst one is giving, another will develop. So it will go for some time in the circle, and when you are giving you will feel that you sometimes do not move forward but let me say, it is in these times when most adjustments are made to the etheric link that joins guide and medium. For you see, it is always an experiment, for none of us, even in the world of Spirit, with our different perception, our deeper understanding of the scheme of things, each medium is as individual as a musical instrument, and it is fashioned in the same way as many others, but will play it's tune differently. It takes great care to tune it, to the right frequency of sound and light, that it may resonate to the highest that it is capable of. Now I say to you, also there is great confusion with your direction, whether you wish to pursue the physical side, or whether you wish to go in to philosophy. What I say to you, why not have both? For you do not need necessarily to choose the pathway, for we will experiment with all that are available to us, in any way that is possible. And if we find that we come and the conditions are more conducive to the physical, then we will not waste this condition, it is like a visit in to the hunting grounds. You may set out to hunt for elk, and you find that all the elk are gone, but you find a great river that is filled with great fish, so it is that you change your perspective, you adapt to the conditions that are most favourable. It is the same for us, and it is difficult for your guides to know in advance, for there are many variables, many factors that affect this. Know that the words that come to you are valid, the words that come you must trust, for there are many that come, many that come from beyond the stars even, to work with you, for you see life does not just remain within this dimension.

 Red Cloud comes forward to you in the guise of human that I was once in this body, but you see I know that there is life and intelligence in many places. The Earth plane is just one of many mansions, where many places that there is consciousness, for it is that you come from a great distance on your journey, young sister, that you come with an energy that is from far away, but it is one that has existed within the Earth but not for many, many moons, for it is an energy that is crystalline, it is a blue light, that comes from your soul, it is one that resonates through many centuries, and it is this that will teach you and take you forward on your pathway.

There has been great loneliness in your life, a feeling of not belonging, a feeling of isolation, but you see this is an inner part of you that remembers your life in the Summerlands of Spirit that recognises your separation from source. Your separation from oneness. And through many difficult relationships, those intimate and those of more friendship, and you have tried to understand this emptiness, and you come to a point in your life now when you can feel that space, and you are surrounded by many workers who come to join you in this, that you may be fulfilled. For all you want is to be useful, to be used , and it is with great joy in my heart that I tell you that you will manifest with your voice, manifest with your demonstration of physical, all alterations of your energy field, that you may bring evidence, evidence of life everlasting in the Spiritual realm. Intent and motivation determines how you evolve. You are beginning a new garden of Spirit. We in Spirit can begin to see the potential in this new group, and it is one of great excitement, for each has his part to play; each is significant and will be used.

It is going to work in a different way with a different energy. It is not going to be in darkness. It will be in light. Gradual increasing of intensity of light, for gone are the days when we hid behind heavy curtains, because this is a world which is open to trickery. We wish to come and show ourselves in ways that have been manifested in the past, without trickery, without darkness. And it is for this reason that we come, to bring the human race in to a deeper level of understanding of your own selves, your own higher selves, that you may see yourselves as you truly are. Not as limited puppets that are unconscious of the ways of your spirit selves, but you know that you have chosen this journey, and you have chosen all of the trials that have gone wrong with this journey, all of those things.

Do you have any questions at this time?"

Jo said, "Yes I do friend. You say about bringing light in to our séance room. Some of the sitters have seen large balls of light already. Is that the beginning of bringing the light?"

"It is a new energy form, it is one that is not from the ectoplasm as in times of old. It is a new form of light that is available to us. As the Earth has increased in frequency over the last two decades, so it is possible for manifestations of Spirit light to show themselves within the physical plane. But at this time the variation in frequency means that only a few that have eyes to see are picking up this frequency of light. It will be, eventually, that all will see, this is the plan you see, this is the plan. And it will be within these lights that faces and forms will appear, and eventually sound will transmit in these spheres also, independent from any sitter, any media.

We wish to demonstrate ourselves without the use of a physical body, for it takes too much energy for this to happen, and we wish to stand free and in our own energy you understand,. It is hoped that when we perfect this, that loved ones will be allowed to use this interface, that will come forward with energies and messages and evidence that will be of use, you understand. This is the way that we wish for things to go, and this is the plan of many of your guides."

Jo exclaimed," Wow! Will this make it a lot safer for those that are in the séance room?"

"It will be, because it will draw its energy not from a physical source, it will draw its energy from the Universe itself. You see, you are working at this time to build a hybrid vortex of energy that links the Spirit Realm and the Earth, and it will become a self-perpetuating source of energy much as you build a fire. Initially, it takes a lot of physical effort to gather wood and to make the spark, but once the fire begins to burn it is easier to put more wood upon the fire. So it is the same with the work that you do. It is beginning to build, and it's by the moon in the winter time, the moon of the hunter, is when you will see a great step forward with your work. The moon of the hunter, it is the time that you call October.

October is a powerful time for your group, for it is at this time that there will be a great moon and clear skies, and you will meet, and the energy is being built for this, so that you will have great evidence. A taste of what is to come, great excitement, and it is important a pen is being placed with you, from your guide."

Jo asked what that meant. "A pen to record what is happening. Do you keep a record of what is happening in your group?"
"We do keep a few, but we're not very good at recording the details."
"It is important, for think of this as a joint experiment between those on the physical plane and those in the world of Spirit. We, too, get very excited when things work, and we must try to remember how we manifested, and what conditions were present, so if both sides are keeping notes it will be easier for the two of us, for we are also human. Although we are Spirit, we get carried away in excitement if we manage to bring through some evidence of manifestation. In that excitement it is difficult for us to remember the conditions that were present prior to that success. So in order to reproduce this, it's very important that people keep records. Each of you should keep a record, not just one person responsible. Each of you must keep a note of things like your physical feeling, whether you feel tired or energised, when you feel sickly. All of these things can be captured so that you can look back to see patterns that are emerging. Some may work better when they are stressed, or with adrenaline. We do not know how these kinds of physical things affect the spirit energy that comes."

Jo then asked, "There are three people in our group currently, would you suggest we increase the number?"

"I believe that eventually there will be three more that will come, for six is a nice number, it is a number that is very powerful in geometry, it is a powerful energy that can be created, but you will not search for these people, they will come in to your laps." Jo then said," How will we know that they are really suitable? We will be a bit nervous about putting our work back".

"You will know, for they will be two that are linked together in relationship, man and woman, and then there will be another woman. Two females and one male. Is that how it is at this time?"

"No, there are two males and myself currently", said Jo.

"There will be one more female, so there will be three and three you understand. That is correct. Not that this is always essential nowadays, for you see that within the Spirit there is both. Anyway, no-one is exclusively male or female in the level of Spirit. But the body is important also at this time, so it is that it carries a certain energy that is needed to build this fire. I sense there will be some kind of gathering of many like minds where you will meet these individuals, and it comes soon, and it feels like a great preparation of light from the world of Spirit, a great convention on both sides of life, and it is here that you will meet those individuals. And you know there will be artistic tendencies with the female, very gentle mediumistic humble lady who will have great artistic traits with her. And you will know her, know the level, for you have experienced those who are not committed, and that is frustrating. Just when things begin to move, people back away from the work, and it is hard to find the commitment , because great patience is required , for it is not exciting every time."

"But it is more than the result that is important. It is important to cultivate the harmony between the sitters, for if you are harmonic with each other and there is love, it will accelerate the development. Harmony is always the most important thing, and more important than ability. If there is ability and not harmony, then you get dissension, and nothing moves forward. It becomes like a dam that stops the flow, and things stagnate."

Jo remarked that the three of them were very harmonious, and had strong connections to each other. Were the spirit team happy with the three?

"Very happy, very happy, and you have powers of reason, emotion, and intellect. There is knowledge in the three that is very important as a corner stone. I feel that there is scientific understanding with one of the three so far, there is a powerful reasoning mind that is very interesting for the spirit team that are gathering to work with you."

"There are scientists from your own historical culture that are involved with the energy on the other side. I feel that it's an American individual that comes, and I feel that the name is Edison I believe. And he comes with knowledge of electrical things and magnetism, and will be part of the experiments as you go forward. So do not doubt that you are on the correct pathway for you. Do not doubt that you should attend this

Conference. For through this, there will be the connections. It may not be that they meet you there, but you will know of them in this place. Your paths will cross, for it is this place that will bring you together. For it has been your choosing for many moons, you have been putting this thought out, of commitment."

Jo then said, "On several occasions, voices have been heard around me, when I've just been relaxing or meditating. How are the team managing to do this?" "It is the use of the spheres. You see the spheres are more than just lights of energy that float in to your plane. They are more cylindrical in form and they allow sound waves to travel in two directions. Light waves and sound waves. So they are in fact more like tubes that link two dimensions. You see them only as light, for the light in the world of Spirit moves at a higher frequency than that in the physical plane, so they illuminate your dimension and they seem quite bright, for light is greater in higher dimensions. So what you perceive as a sphere of light is more like a hole or cylindrical form, a vortex, and when that comes close to you there are voices that come with it. For there are many that wish to connect with you from your own memories, your own loved ones. One very strong presence of a female is very close to you, and feels very protective, motherly towards you, but it may be a grandparent. She was quite small and frail when she was in the body. She is very excited with your work. I do not see this, I see merely her form at this time. Let me see. I feel it begins with an M sounding name, like May or Mary, something like this sound, the name that comes. She is small in build, and she comes forward with fine china cups and I feel she shows me in cups there are grounds in the cups and she shows me this and she laughs, with great glee at this, and she is eager to show you that she understands your work.

Jo sent her love, and Red Cloud said that her love was already there my dear.

"She tells me there is a problem with her lower limb". Jo said she thought the leg referred to her great grandmother. If that's the case, she would not have actually met her.

"She is a strong personality. She is part of the helpers who are working with you, out of your band of guides. You see your family are very eager that you are in this work.

Jo said, "My family in Spirit are, my family on earth are not."

"Your family in Spirit are very eager that you are in this work. For you see, there have been others in your line that have been in this in this work in the past, but not for maybe a hundred years. I feel the time of the Victorian era, when Spiritualism was new in this country. That was when you had parts of your family who were involved in this. Of course it was frowned upon by other parts of your family, there is much fear there, and she tells me also of the situation with the firewater, the alcohol problem that has troubled your family. I don't know if it's of this time or a past event."

Jo confirmed that it was a past event.

"Well it caused a great division, and much hurt. He wishes to say that this is now resolved and those involved are evolving in the world of Spirit."
Jo said she was pleased to hear that.
"So it is with great love that she comes to you, and she tells me that she has tried to speak to you, she has been one of the voices that have been heard".
Jo said ahhh!

"She will come to you in your group, she tells me she has shown herself, she has been seen." Jo said excellent.
" It was her who came forward to you". Jo said that it made her very happy to know that, thank you.
"Are there any further questions?"
A section concerning the other sitter followed, and after that Jo thanked Red Cloud very much for speaking with them.
"It has been my honour, and there will be times, if it is permissible, that I may come to join your team to observe how you are progressing".
Jo said he would be most welcome.

"It is you see that we all meet up as you do in your conferences on the Earth plane, guides in the Spirit World also meet up, and we are working in a hierarchy much as you are on Earth plane. There are very wise teachers, and there are the humble workers such as myself, who come just to pass on observations in whatever way is possible.
So it is that I leave you with these thoughts and I breathe in to your energy fields the smoke of my ancestors, that it may strengthen your resolve to your

work, that you may build a lodge that is worthy of Great Spirit, that you may bring great love and great healing in to this Earth, for it surely needs it at this time, more so than it has ever done, so the work will go forward like a wave, out in to your communities where it is needed. It is my pleasure and I leave you with these thoughts."

Red Cloud was thanked as he left, and the medium returned to full consciousness.

On the 6th July 2006, about three months after what Red Cloud had said about the light spheres or tubes, a photograph was taken with a disposable camera, and it showed an "extra" not seen at the time, a light beam coming down on Jo while she was quietly reading, and also an anomaly in her bag. . (See Chapter 9).

This was followed on 12th July by another strange occurrence, which did not happen to Jo, but was about her and the circle. It was through her friend, who she described as a most wonderfully gifted platform and trance medium. The friend, Michael, phoned Jo, just after she had taken part in her circle sitting. She was vibrating on her leg, and Mick immediately said, "You spoke in trance tonight, it was a man, Jesus Christ I have to put the phone down". Jo was a little confused, but he phoned back 5 minutes later, apologising, saying nothing like that had ever happened to him before. He said that Jo's guide was still with her, which she confirmed was correct. He said if he came that close again he would have to put the phone down again, as he felt he was going into trance himself. (He was driving his black cab at the time).

He said, "He is telling me that he spoke through you again tonight, and I don't know how you can handle his energy, he is much larger in bodily size and strength too, he said he is telling me about the scientists that are working with you, and what they are going to do, oh my God, they are all going to show themselves standing in front of a light, including a little girl, who carries a toy with her." Micky then spoke about the light beam photograph, and he said that the experts won't be able to explain it, because it is the new energy showing itself. This turned out to be correct, about the photograph.

Chapter 6: Second Paul Case trance reading

About a year later, a lot had been going on in the
séances and in the home, and Jo took the opportunity
to have another reading with Paul Case. She wanted
to confirm all that had happened, and to see what else
lay ahead. She had questions relating to things she
didn't understand, so went to try to get an
explanation.

"The Spirit is strong. They build great fire for us this
day. Much activity, and energy. As I look in to the
faces that come to link with us, there are many old
and wise Spirit guides, but there are also family
members, those who have worked in this field, you
understand. (Yes I do). For I see darkened room,
heavy curtains, and a female who was a very
powerful medium upon the Earth plane, who comes
to congratulate at this time, for there has been
progression with the building of this independent
voicebox with you. (Yes). And it feels as if the Spirit
team that work with your group are delighted at the
changes that have come and passed (Yes) for there is
an energy of great commitment going forward, they
tell me. And it feels as if it has projected you in
confidence (Yes) for as well as this physical
development, there is also an inner healing that has
taken place for the separation within your own
emotional body, has centred into a place of
understanding and peace, that you feel more settled
within yourself. So it is that when you are calm, when
you are at peace, it is as if the energy of Spirit can
manifest much more simply around you, for it is like

you are the eye of the hurricane, the eye of the storm, and within this central point there is peace and harmony, you understand. (Yes I do).

So it is that there is much communication, for they are working on two levels with you, two levels. One is conscious, and one is unconscious. For they show me words that come, that you are aware of, and you share these thoughts, these communications, and it is almost as if you are upon a platform, or demonstrating in this way, and I feel that it is something that is very close, if not manifesting at this time, you understand.
(I don't understand that, I'm sorry).
It is a communication, it is a conscious communication, through you from Spirit, but it is something that will be shared in public forum, so it is not a private home circle you understand (OK) so it will be a small group of people who are hand-picked and trustworthy, and you will begin to speak and Spirit will take over the proceedings. (OK thank you) and this comes further in the future time but very soon, very soon, for it is as if many such as you are converging at this time, it is almost as if there is a place of great learning that comes together that you will go to learn, but will actually be used to teach, you understand, and it feels like some place, like some kind of convention or gathering of many different mediums and abilities.

You will be in this vicinity for but only for one part of this you understand, just to experience what you wish to experience, for there is also as we go forward, as we close the door on the past events, it is almost as if there has been an awakening of your own confidence with your discernment of Spirit, and of those who have sought to restrict you in your growth, you understand. (Yes I do) So it is that you move forward with clarity of consciousness, but you do not judge them, you merely sidestep the situation (Yes that's true) gracefully, without damaging their egos, for you see they would not understand. They are only concerned with controlling, and keeping things in their own circle, you understand. (Yes I do).

I feel that there are many things that move.This lady from the Spirit world that comes, I am not sure whether this is a grandmother figure for you, but she's very much matriarch in the family you understand. (Yes) I see very small dwelling places very closely connected and intertwined, and many family members that were involved in this interest, you understand.(Yes) It has missed a generation, for she tells me it is not in your parents' generation you understand, but has manifested in you.

For I can see many items of divination, such as the teacup and things like this, and a time when there was great fear within the community, a time of wartime conditions, and there was much Spirit work that was undertaken in these times. But she shows that there is recognition of your abilities. Are there memories of your connection with this lady in the physical plane? (I'm not sure, I believe I know the ladies name, she's given it to me, but I don't know whether she's a grandmother or not.)

For I feel that she's a matriarch of the community, and feels protective and motherly over many people. There is a quite disjointed feeling as she explores this thought, it is almost as if there is displacement of your family lines, you understand, a feeling of adoption (yes you're correct) for it feels as if the people who have raised you would not necessarily have been blood, or would have been removed you understand, distant in biology but closer spiritually. (Yes). And it is with this feeling of much love that she comes, but you have for many years felt alone and unworthy, for it's a time of great celebration in Spirit that you now value yourself. You understand this.(I do understand that). And it is for many times in your trail in the past that you have attracted to you the same lesson of defeat and being squashed to the ground. (Yes that's true). But now it is no longer necessary, for you have risen like a phoenix from the flames, with your spirituality broken and exposed. So it is that some times in the physical flame as you know that we have to lose all things, to find what is true to us. (Yes) So it is that there has been this breaking down of your outer life to reveal the inner life of Spirit, which is the true nature and the true peace that comes.

And I feel as if there is great activity within the Spirit team, for there are many with intellect of sciences within the team, you understand (Yes) and they are very excited about light that they bring. They have managed to transcend the barrier between our side and your side, they have transcended a barrier, and things will advance more speedily now. (Fantastic!)

For it is the theme of the old ways, but it is not to be hidden behind darkness for ever. For the light will be so clear that all will see the transfiguration, the materialisation, the voice, and at this time there are two channels, it is almost as if there is an echo for the voices used in your vocal chords, but it is mirrored in the ectoplasmic voice box, you understand? (Yes I do). So you find as your experiment proceeds that there will be two voices, one through you and one through the independent communication. Do not be alarmed, this is something that has to be built first. They have to build your physicality to extend an etheric duplicate, in the space between our dimensions. So it is exciting, and all according to plan! (Wonderful!)

For there is much philosophy, there is much evidence, that needs to come, for you, in your dream, wish to demonstrate evidence from the horse's mouth, so to speak. (Yes that's true). This is your dream, but you see that physical mediums are very rare, mediums that are of the calibre that is required for the dedication, for the humility, for the right balance of qualities, very rare upon the Earth plane at this time. So you will find that many Spirit teams will have their own agendas, so it is that you may feel the main thrust of your work will be individual evidence from loved ones, but if there is an opportunity for healing, for physical operations, of healing, then they will use you in this way. (That's fantastic). For you see there are surgeons that are part of this team, there are those who you call physicists, there are medical practitioners, there are people from my own race, there are philosophical individuals from many cultures, there is one who is Oriental, who shows himself in the smoke of your team.

And there are also many children that come. There is one boy and one girl who are very close to the front of this circle. They both seem to come from maybe 200 years previous, maybe Victorian times. The boy is very cheeky, very much fun, and comes with memories of being crushed, or trapped in some way, for I see tracks upon the street, and maybe what you call railway or tram, a vehicle, and there is some accident, he cuts between the tracks very quickly and nimbly, but was passed over to Spirit at a very young age. The girl is slightly older, very upper class, in comparison to the boy. And she is very well spoken and helps those communicators to operate the voice box. For she has perfect diction and will be waiting to speak and even sing, she tells me. (Lovely!) For she is very pretty, very blonde ringlets, very pretty girl. (Excellent). And she passed over with an illness, a wasting condition, where she had withered limbs in this condition, but she is vibrant in Spirit of course and it is necessary for children to be part of this work, for they have the ability to be imaginative and flexible where an adult would not. Even though they manifest in the Spirit world as adult beings, they choose to reflect their persona in the childlike aspect of themselves. For this gives great clarity and innocence to the proceedings. So they are part of this work (Excellent), so is there some question at this time?

(We've seen various lights, one of the sitters in particular keeps seeing a face within the light, is that so, can you confirm that with the team?)

I see…an elderly gentleman that comes forward, and I feel there is some kind of facial hair that shows (Yes that's right) let me see. This is interesting, for pointed beard almost as if there is…what is this round the neck like a kind of decorative collar, I have seen this on individuals from Shakespearian times (Yes) and this person comes forward from this era, it is part also of the voice for this person is not from this era . They correct me, they are from your time, but they would have been a person who played characters from this era, so it would have been an actor you understand, and it is all to manifest and strengthen and reinforce the projection of sound through this facility. (Fantastic). So it is that many will come and show themselves as they begin to shape the template that is being formed. It is almost as if around you some of your own life force has been borrowed, and placed in a kind of vacuum so to speak, so it is that you may have felt very tired or depleted of late. Do not be alarmed for this is not like the physical mediumship of old, they will not deplete your health you understand. (I'm not concerned at all, I trust all my guides) So it will be a hybrid, a new aspect of physical mediumship, for instead of using solely ectoplasmic form of energy, they attempt to create a new space, a new energy.
(Ah that leads me to a question. When one of our guides materialised in the room, she informed us that they had used the voice through an ectoplasmic

voicebox , but when she materialised it was using the new energy) .

This is true, for there are two channels at work here. If you imagine that your dimension is here, and between the two there is almost a membrane that separates our two dimensions, your ectoplasm is used for matter that passes between. So sound, thought, thought waves, translated in to sound vibration, pass through this membrane. Whereas what is happening with the materialisation is they are taking energy from Spirit and they are bending reality to create a space of Spirit in the physical plane, so instead of a clear line of dimension, there is a bulge forming, and this bulge uses your essence but it is filled with the light of this new energy. And it is you will find, if we were to describe how we see your energy field, it is like clear plastic with pockets forming around it, almost like what you call packing bubble, bubble wrap, and within those bubbles is Spirit manifesting but that is existing in the physical plane, so it is almost borrowed space (Yes) but as it is enclosed within this pocket it does not take so much energy to manifest. (Cool.) Which means the sessions will be longer and more communication. (Which is great. Can I ask something else? When I go to bed at night, I get lots of dripping all over me, in the séance room lots of dripping. Is this from the new energy, or is it from the ectoplasm?)

It is part of both, again for you see the bubble wrap if you like is formed from ectoplasm, and this is permanently outside of yourself now, it is not in the old ways of ectoplasm, it is extracted from the medium then returned. In your instance, what they are attempting to do is to create these permanent fixtures so to speak that are independent, but are of your essence. So what is happening with the dripping sensation it is the flow, the overflow of Spirit energy that is giving back to you. For you see you have with you a very famous nurse, or scientist, who was a great mind in Spirit, and she is very interested in the biology of your physical body and your spiritual body, and she wants to ensure that once this energy is used that they return to you the surplus in readiness for the next part of your journey. So though you may feel initially depleted in the forming of these capsules, any energy that is formed to fill these spaces that is surplus is given to you and to your circle, and it manifests as drips in to your energy field. (OK that's cool!) It's almost like condensation , spiritual condensation. (That's cool, I have spiritual condensation! I have another question, about my head. A glowing head is the only way I can really describe it. I have a certain place on my head that burns quite hot at times. Do we know what this is? It isn't a medical problem.)

It is where you are moving outside of yourself. They are taking you further from yourself and there is a lack of consciousness at this time, so they are making a doorway so you can come in to your body to witness what is happening, so there are times that your consciousness needs to be moved aside. That is why they create this, almost a portal. It is what you call a chakra point, but it is not really something that you must open or close. It is something your Spirit

team is working on, but something will come over the
face. They are attempting to create a face, a mask,
that will pour over yourself. This is, I believe,
transfiguration, but I feel that you may, as well as the
voice, you will have independent face that matches
the voice. (Oh wicked!) But it will not be animated,
it will be, they show me a photographic plate, so it
will be the sound that comes, but the person will be
projected in this space, (Ah lovely!) but it will not be
your face changing , it will be overlay, an overlay, on
top of your own face. So from the side it will look
like a veil that hangs, you see.

They wish to provide absolute evidence, so for a
person who is unclear that is coming through in the
voice the person in the sitting will know the face that
is shown. (Excellent, that's fantastic) For you cannot
dispute your own eyes, (No you cannot!) and many
times communicators try and struggle with the
ectoplasmic voice box to bring their own personality
and evidence through, for they are emotional or it is
new to them, so this is a way that they can confirm
two levels at one time. (Awesome!) This is what is
being projected forward.

The crown is where they remove you from your
wakening state in to the deep trance condition, but at
this time you step down, step up, step down, step up
you understand this. (Yes I do). You are still mainly
here, but occasionally you go, and when you go it is
to make room for the entrance of greater spirit energy
you understand (Yes I do). For you know there is no
involvement, you know you are not creating this from

your subconscious (I know that) for it is beyond that doubt in your own mind. But it feels sometimes as if you wish to witness all things, and you will, but they need for you to be used in Spirit as well. (I'm quite happy with that, that's fine. I've seen many beautiful things). For you see as well as being taken in to a place of healing like I do with my boy, they will wish for you to be co-ordinating the spirit people that come through. For you are training with us to be a Spirit guide yourself in this lifetime (Gosh am I?) You have been apprenticed I believe is the word in this lifetime, so it is exciting you see, for the layers of Spirit, and the layers of the physical plane, always seem so far apart, but as time goes forward in your lifetime those responsibilities will cross, because we will walk among you in solid form (Excellent) and it is something that has been on the Earth plane many centuries in the past in more innocent times, before the air waves were filled with many frequencies. So it is that you will find this will interfere with your work too, electrical disturbances, even climate conditions, but you will find when it is very cold and clear and frosty there will be good evidence.

(Oh lovely is it this year?) It is, for I see you stepping out of your dwelling place and looking up in to the frosty sky, and the stars shine down, and then you go in to your place of meditation and it is wonderful energy. (Excellent) .

What is very urgent what is very urgent is. Is there a sense in your circle of drawing closer together in physicality, have you filled in gaps in the circle?

(We've recently had another new sitter come). This would make sense for it feels like there was a necklace with beads and there were gaps in the necklace, and now it tightens and is very integrated (Cool, so the team is happy with everyone we've got?) Very very good feeling that comes (Excellent) straight away there is a gelling and humour and respect and trust (Yes) which is so essential for this work as you know.

(We've had a fair bit of direct voice but they don't seem to be able to maintain it at the moment. Are they adjusting the voice box?)

It is as I say, you imagine the spirit team sitting around their camp fire discussing the priority of the day. You have the physicist that wishes to bring investigation of matter and molecules, you have the medical fraternity who wishes to bring advancement of healing and physical manipulation of physical cells of the body, and you have those from my area who try to oversee all of these things, mediate between what is most urgent, and at this time what is very urgent upon the Earth plane is the understanding and evidence. (Absolutely!)

So, evidence, but evidence on its own does not help people to move on, for sometimes evidence alone can become intoxicating for a person who is grieving, so it is that we as spirit guides try to bring many irons to the fire, so that there is learning and education and wisdom. For evidence alone will place ointment upon that hurt, but it does not help that person to explore their own spirituality. It may be a catalyst for some, but you see from our perspective we want all Spirit to

be one, in thought and consciousness, whether you
are incarnate or in Spirit. So there is an agenda, to
educate the sitters, the mediums, to bring the truth if
the joy of Spirit, the joy of communion between our
worlds, this is what is forgotten.

Forget the sensational, the mediums who wish to be
placed on pedestals, living in mansions, forget the
psychic level, forget all of this. It is the true cause, of
spirituality, the truth that life goes on, the wisdom
that you do not have to wait to be in Spirit to
understand the dimension that is waiting for you in
the Summerlands of Spirit. You do not need to wait to
be told, each and every individual can embrace reality
from any condition, as there are many irons in the fire
at this time. So there is a certain, not argument but
debate, within your Spirit team, and sometimes they
will prioritise and they will say you are depleted, you
need rest, so we do not fill this bubble wrap today, we
give her a rest today. But you also see Spirit, do you
not? (Yes I do.) Sometimes much information can
come in this way, many levels, all have their
worthiness.
(Absolutely!) Are there any more questions? (I don't
think there are actually).

It is so exciting for an old man to step in to the smoke
of your fire, for your fire of course is a symbol of
your Spirit journey and the work you have
contributed, and it is you see burning brightly and
many souls come to be warmed in this enlightening,
in this excitement, for you see your spirit team are in
the centre, they're arranged in the outer dimension,

in an arena or amphitheatre, as you would
d many are invited to come, and watch and
me would be future mediums, to wait and
project again in to an Earthly condition. Spirits that
are waiting will learn from you, for you are a pioneer
of your day (Thankyou) , you are one of others that
are placed on all continents at this time. (Excellent).
But you see, the heart of spirit is within this small
green land, for you see in many other countries there
is not the experience.

But you will eventually carry what you have
developed in to other places, you understand, and you
will be willing to do so. (I'm more than happy to
share anything).
For it is such a wonderful gift you understand. (It's
lovely.Lovely being very close).
And there is much support for you, much support, and
I feel in your personal life also things seem to be
somehow crystallizing in to a peaceful scenario, it is
almost as if there is disorder without makes disorder
within (Yes) so to create this peace and time for
yourself , to reflect, is very essential. For you see, as
an instrument, you are easily disturbed, and vibrate
like the strings of a violin. If there is disturbance in
your vicinity, it can upset your balance very easily,
but you are protected, but where we cannot protect
you of course is where you allow those to come and
disrupt (Yes) and that of course is something only
you can learn. And we feel in Spirit at this time that
you have demonstrated great strength in this level of
late, in saying no you understand (Yes) without being
obnoxious, without being unkind or judgemental.

But it is a very difficult gift to embrace for you see, as a giver, and a healer, and a medium, you wish to save everybody, and of course as you grow in your own spirituality you realise. Like the gardener, you might plant 100 seeds, but only 70 will grow, for 30 will lie dormant for they are not ready. So it is the wisdom of the gardener that can walk away from the flowerbed, and know that those seeds are in the soil and will germinate at a later stage. So people in your vicinity, who do not understand your passion for the work, who do not understand or maybe even chastise you for this, they are the seeds that lie dormant in the soil and walk away gently, knowing that they will be nurtured and safe and will eventually, as will others, move on. The sun will reach them you understand. So it is always a beautiful image to look at Nature for within all Nature is a reflection of all the wisdom the Great Spirit has to offer for all of us. For we are all mirrors, but great excitement (Lovely thanks) .

And I feel as if there are such a lot of old generation physical mediums that are part of your team also. (That's fantastic, as I have much to learn) . And it is they who are wishing to evolve this mediumship , for you see the old physical mediumship has become incompatible with the vibration of planet Earth at this time. Earth no longer works at that low vibration, for everything accelerates and evolves, we evolve in Spirit, the Earth evolves, so the mechanism of communication must also evolve. It is akin to the frequency of a radio communication.

You cannot always turn on AM band when FM band is more clear and available. It is similar in mediumship, and as the Earth has moved in to higher vibration of consciousness it opens up the compatibility for this new energy, that will sustain itself, that will bring it's own light, it's manifestations, and it may be transparent at times, it may be swirling colours on a soap bubble, but it take form and solidity, it will take form. But you know that these forms will touch you, not vice versa, you know this don't you? So wait to be invited to touch them. And there will be also I am told an experiment, with not seeing, but feeling.

They will bring different textures to the group, some will feel the silk, some will feel plant matter, woollen blankets, that sort of thing , so they bring form in touch in physicality, but it will not have visibility at that time. Then they combine the two threads of frequency to create the holographic, that is solid and visible. So it is almost like a hologram. Like a projection of smoke and mirrors as they say. So that will not be easy to touch, for it may disturb as rippling the surface of water, distort the image. So as they develop this, they will reach out to those in the group.

(Can I ask one final question? The main guide that has come through and materialised several times already encourages us to touch him back. Does that mean he's slightly more developed than the others who come and materialise?)

This is true, for you see what happens it is as a guide comes they create a template, so he would have developed one of your little bubbles, so to speak . One of your little spaces is his, and has almost become self-recognising as he steps in, so it is not easy to disrupt it so he will invite you to touch. But others that come for the first time you will help them more by not touching. (Absolutely!) So you understand this, but they will not be allowed to invite if it causes any damage. So they're directed by the Spirit team in the same way that you are.

But they wish to bring more detail, not just shapes and shadows. They want specific facial features for example, not just figures, so look out for this. (Excellent).
Very exciting time. (Very exciting thank you so much).
It is always such a long time in coming, physical mediumship development, but for you it's been with you since childhood, so you have psychokinetic abilities, you have always been surrounded by the raps and taps and movement of Spirit but not understood this. How marvellous! Well we wish you all the best in your development, know that you are on an exciting journey but will in the fullness of time demonstrate this, to not necessarily great Halls, but small groups of hand-picked individuals. But there will always be a pattern. For it will be started with fun, it will move on to evidence, then there will be philosophy, then it will end with fun. (Lovely) That is how they wish to make the agenda for you. (And that sounds just perfect).

So there is always a little wisdom thrown in to broaden the minds of the sitters, for it is that which gives true peace really. So it has been my honour to look in to the smoke for you this day. (Thank you so much)
And we know that you have a difficult journey and we will make sure that you find a nice place to stop to replenish yourself on the way home on your journey. So I now leave you with the blessings of my ancestors as I breathe in to you the smoke of my pipe, to give you strength and fortitude that you may always follow your heart. For to follow your heart means that you are worthy of the work that is in front of you. That is all we ask. It is always my honour to come and I leave you with this thought."

The trance readings were gradually fulfilled as time went on. During a séance, this photo of Jo was taken in dim white light:

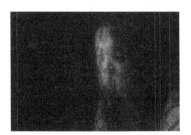

Extract from Red Cloud's prophecy:

'It is something your Spirit team is working on, but something will come over the face. They are attempting to create a face, a mask, that will pour over yourself. This is, I believe, transfiguration, but I feel that you may, as well as the voice, you will have independent face that matches the voice. (Oh wicked!) But it will not be animated, it will be, they show me a photographic plate, so it will be the sound that comes, but the person will be projected in this space, (Ah lovely!) but it will not be your face changing , it will be overlay, an overlay, on top of your own face. So from the side it will look like a veil that hangs, you see. They wish to provide absolute evidence, so for a person who is unclear that is coming through in the voice the person in the sitting will know the face that is shown.'

Chapter 7: Further circle advances

Meanwhile, other seances had produced interesting
results. On 2ⁿᵈ April 2007, the circle sat on a Friday
night. They sat around the wooden table as usual,
holding hands, and the guides were invited to draw
close. On the table were about 20 sheets of A4 paper,
a pen, a bell, a whistle, some wooden rings, and a
handkerchief. The trumpet was placed on the
floor.The spare chairs had been placed inside the old
cabinet, along with chalk and a tambourine.

After a couple of minutes, the table started to move,
tilt, and then levitate a few inches off the ground. It
was then brought back down, and again rose but
much higher this time, staying in the air for about 10
seconds, before gently descending.

The handkerchief was knotted and dropped into Jo's
lap. She, as normal, spoke with the guides,
encouraging direct voice, in the hope that evidence
would be forthcoming. They heard some of the
wooden rings on the table being moved and then
being tapped together. Jo asked if Spirit could try to
link them, and then give them to a sitter.Andrew and
Jo were touched by a small hand which belonged to a
spirit child. It gripped them firmly on their hands and
arms. The child standing next to Jo made a sound, it
was very tinny at first, that's the only way it could be
described, and then the child started to whistle, it
grew louder and louder in strength. Jo was feeling
very light headed, but along with everyone else
continued to encourage the child with the sound. The
whistle was continuous for 3 - 4 minutes, and unlike
anyone in the physical body who would have to

draw in air after a short time, the child did not. The sound did not stop, even for a second . Jo asked the child to move away from her, and as she did so the whistle grew weaker in sound. Jo asked her to come back toher side, and again the same level of sound flowed from her. This was the first independent direct voice of strength and length that the circle had experienced.

An ex-circle member, Alec, guested in the circle on 12th April 2007. He was now living abroad. This is his report on the sitting.

"What a wonderful evening! The circle was opened with an invitation to the guides to draw close to us. I welcomed my old friends, having not been close to them for some time.We sat around the large circular wooden table in the middle of the seance room. Placed upon it was A4 paper, a pen, the trumpet and a bell.

The first thing we became aware of was, the paper being scrunched and balls thrown accurately at all of us. I personally got hit by 3 of them squarely on my forehead. I was amazed at the sound of the screwing of the paper though, it was different, unusual, like not of this world almost. I know you will all think that's a mad statement to make, but its a true one. We experienced, (and I for the first time), the table levitating, it was interesting, the height and speed at which it levitated.

We heard sound, although quiet, but definitely someone was trying to speak, everyone encouraged the voice. Jo and Richard were seated with another sitter between them. Both at the same time reported having solid warm hands placed on their heads. We were all seated holding hands, so we knew the hands did not belong to any of the circle sitters. We asked if it was the same spirit person touching Jo and Richard, and was told 'No', so we had two solid hands belonging to two seperate spirit forms, quite remarkable. They seemed to be having difficulties in speaking though, so they wrote their names on the paper for us instead, 'William' and 'Kathleen'.

At the end of the sitting, I gathered the paper together, and imprinted on to one piece of A4 was the imprint of a face, and it was signed in the bottom right hand corner by 'William'. I just couldn't believe it."

The sittings continued, and on 13th May 2007 another notable event occurred. Jason was not present and Richard took his seat. After the opening prayer, within a few minutes Kathleen came close, and gave them a wonderful trumpet display. She then opened a new packet of plasticine which was lying on the table, and they could hear her rolling and patting the plasticine. They asked if she was making another model from it. The answer was yes, and it took her a few minutes to complete. She then picked up the bag which had contained the plasticine, and started to rub it together at high speed, creating light from the static, for several minutes. She invited the circle to take a ten minute refreshment break, which they did, and when the light was put on they saw a stunning model of a canoe, complete with man and oars.

They restarted for the second session with an opening prayer, and Kathleen returned to give another wonderful display with the trumpet. Jo asked if it would be possible for her to write them a message, and she did, which they found at the end of the sitting. It read, "Kathleen loves Jo, Callum, and Richard".

Jo asked if she could try speaking again to them. The trumpet hovered mid-air in front of her, and she said through the trumpet "Yes", then "Hello". She then appeared very excited and continued to smack the trumpet hard on the table.

Kathleen then pulled the table away from Jo, and then pulled her on her chair towards the blacked out window. They heard the cable tie being notched, and it was placed round Jo's foot. She then took Jo's ring off her finger and slipped it on to her toe!

Jo was feeling very light-headed, then Kathleen stroked her fingers through Jo's hair.

Jo's head was feeling dizzy, and then she was lifted on her chair up in the air for a few seconds. This was another amazing night, thanks to Kathleen and the rest of the team.

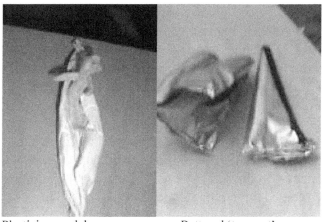

Plasticine model   Battered 'trumpet'

The next sitting on 15th May was also very successful, with the sitters in their usual chairs. After the opening prayer, the trumpet began to move, swaying across the table, and then up in to the air. They asked if it was Kathleen, "Yes" was the answer. She gave them another wonderful trumpet display, then she opened some new plasticine, made another wonderful model boat, and signed it.

Jo's head felt that it was glowing, then suddenly Callum was lifted in to the air, about two feet off the ground. He stayed there a few seconds, was brought down, then lifted again for a few seconds. Kathleen showed great control with these levitations, as she had done previously when Jo had been taken in to the air.

The spirit team were thanked, and they closed with a prayer.

The circle continued without interruptions, and with dedication. Records were faithfully kept and are available for evidence of the circle's progress.

In July 2008, Jo's adoptive father, Raymond, passed over to Spirit side, which was very traumatic for Jo and the family, as they had been so close. But it was not the end for Jo's Dad, as events were to prove. An interesting set of coincidences occurred by his passing. Jo's adoptive father and her grandfather both died on 28th July. They died 28 years apart, in 1980 and 2008. Both died at 6.07 am. And both died on Mondays. Jo doesn't believe in coincidences, and this one seemed quite remarkable to her.

Chapter 8: Direct voice at death-bed

Jo's father had suffered from leukemia, and had showed much courage throughout his illness. The family found it an agony to watch him suffer so much, unable to take his pain away from him. Her father was an atheist, he absolutely refused to accept there was any form of afterlife, believing that once you're dead, you're dead, that's it, black hole, absolute nothing. That was OK for Jo. She knew differently!

As her father lay unconscious in his last few days, she did begin to worry that his rejection of any belief would cause him difficulty. All sorts of things went through her mind, even thinking, at one point, that he might refuse to go where he had to go, rejecting a loved one who was there to collect him. Jo absolutely knew of the afterlife, so why these thoughts went through her head, she had no idea. However, their family was to receive ultimate proof that her worries were unfounded.

Two days before her father passed, at about 1am in the morning, Jo was called to her father's bedside. Her younger sister and two of her brothers, along with her mother, were there. Her father had suffered a stroke, and after a while her mother retired to bed, with a promise that she would be awakened if there was any change with Dad.
They had been quietly sitting along the length of the bed for about 30 minutes, none of them saying a word to each other, when to Jo's left, a lady's voice

called out, "'Ray". Jo's sister looked at Jo in total surprise, and said, " I have just heard a woman". Jo said, " Yes, I did too".

A brother, who was sat between them, acknowledged her also, then the voice came again, this time from Jo's right. She called his name again. The youngest brother, who was sitting near Dad's feet, went a horrid colour of grey. He was muttering under his breath, that although he had some belief in an afterlife, he really didn't want to experience anything and would they please stop!

Again the voice came, from in front of them. Jo's sister asked if she could see the woman. At first she couldn't, but then the woman appeared to her floating above her Dad, her face very close to his. Jo knew who it was instantly, although she appeared a lot younger than she had previously seen her on the earth plane. It was his mother. A moment later she called to her son again, this time using his full name, "'Raymond'", but also asked him to go with her. They were all transfixed. The feeling of love in the room was intoxicating. Their Dad, who had been unconscious for over 24 hours at this point, slowly opened his eyes, and after a few seconds his eyes widened almost in astonishment, before he slowly closed them again.

His mother was not going to be defeated. She moved to his side, and started calling him again, speaking into his right ear. Six times in all she spoke, clearly audible to all in the room. Jo's older brother encouraged her father to go with her, reassuring him it was OK to leave.

Jo had to return home the following day, to continue preparations for her daughter's wedding, which was only four days away. During the early hours of the following morning, her mother, and her two youngest sisters, were at his bedside. Dad opened his eyes when Mum was gently kissing his forehead. He uttered two words to her, "Crossing over", before smiling, and taking his last breath. Jo believed that he wanted her Mum to know, that he knew there was an afterlife, after all.

Six weeks later, Jo held a seance at her mother's house. Earlier in the evening they had gone to scatter his ashes at his favourite fishing spot, so it was an incredibly emotional day. Not long into the seance, her father spoke briefly through the ectoplasmic voice box to her mother. He had also made his hand solid, and was holding Jo's mother's hand. His voice was full of emotion, and he could barely get his words out. But they knew without doubt it was him. Not bad for a man who had had no belief system throughout his life!

Shortly after Jo's Dad passed, at the end of July, 2008, Jo's sister and her mum asked her if she would sit in a family circle to be held at her mother's house. Jo agreed. Sitters were Jo, mum, Jo's sister, and a very close friend.
On their first sitting, which was eventful with a small amount of direct voice, they closed the circle, and retired to bed. The close family friend slept on the sofa, as she had to leave very early the next morning, to get home to care for the children, so that her

husband could leave for work. Jo found it extremely hard to sleep, as someone was stamping quite hard up and down the landing. Eventually, when she had decided to get out of bed to deal with the situation, the noise stopped.

The following morning Jo's mother was up first at about 8.30am. She went through to the conservatory to let the cat out, however, she discovered the door was locked, which alarmed her somewhat, as it was the only door that had the key left in it's lock in order for their friend to leave. Believing she must have over-slept, her mother rushed through to the living room to wake the friend, only to discover that she had gone.

Jo and her sister came downstairs shortly afterwards, to find Mum puzzling over the locked door. Jo then started asking who had been stamping up and down the landing, as it had kept her awake and she was still feeling tired. They both said they had not heard a sound, which Jo found curious as her mother always slept with her bedroom door wide open.

Jo's sister decided to phone the friend. She asked her which door she had left the house by, and the reply was, the conservatory door of course, it was the only one with a key to let herself out. Jo's sister explained what had happened, and was met by a stunned silence. The friend then said, "Well, I have had little sleep with all that stamping going on last night, but I definitely know which door I left by, and no of course I did not lock it after I left, the key was left in the lock on the inside."

The circle experienced a personal message to Jo's mother at a later circle. She had visited from Somerset, and sat as a guest on a Sunday . They took a dictaphone into the seance room. Some time after the circle had begun, they heard deep breathing from a male. They were hopeful that whoever it was would speak through direct voice, but after a while he seemed to be struggling somewhat. Jo encouraged him to leave a message, along with his name, on the recorder instead.

The circle closed some 20 minutes later, and after thanking their spirit team, and closing the circle in the usual manner, they retired to the dining room to enjoy refreshments. Jo rewound the tape and they sat listening as they sipped their coffee. About halfway through the recording, a man's voice cut in and said,'Ray'.......followed by ' I reallyyyyyyy love you'. Her mother was beside herself with emotion, as indeed Jo was too. Her Dad 'Ray' had only been in the spirit realms since July. It was remarkable how quickly he was learning how to communicate with them, but of course it is the Love link that strengthens that connection.

Chapter 9:   Outside the seance room.

Phenomena always seemed to play a large part of
Jo's life outside the seance room too.The more recent
had been the direct voice, but there were
manifestations in several other ways too.
One example involved her daughter. She was doing a
photography project at school, and had one of those
disposal cameras. She walked around the house,
snapping pictures of family members who were just
chilling out. Jo was sat in the dining/family room with
her head stuck in a book. She took little notice of her
daughter's activities, because natural, not posed,
pictures were wanted.

A week later, Jo collected the pictures from the
developer, and was quite astounded, on reviewing
them, that one picture taken of her had what can only
be described as a beam of light showing, as an
addition to the scene. It ran straight down at an angle,
ending at her shoulder. It was not like any of the other
many photographs she had seen, with orbs and
strange mists. This was perfectly formed, and looked
similar to a torch beam coming down from the
ceiling.

Jo's friend was so fascinated by this picture, that she
asked if they could go to London, and get several
experts to give their opinion on it. The following
week, they travelled to London, and took the
photograph to three different experts, asking them if
their were any natural cause or development problem
that could have caused this beam to appear. They

immediately ruled out exposure problems, hair on the lens, and all the normal occurrences that at times take place. Each said individually that, whatever it was, was in the room when the picture was taken, because the beam of light did not extend onto the negative outside of the actual picture, even though the beam had not been seen by them at the time. There was no window for light to come in, and no lights switched on, as it had been the middle of the afternoon. This photo remains a mystery, to this day.

As well as the light beam, there are other puzzles connected with this photo. Jo is sure she was reading a book, and her fingers are in a position suggesting she was holding a book as she looks down, but the book cannot be seen in the photo. Also, poking out of Jo's bag on the sofa can be seen 'something' coloured orange, which Jo is sure was not there at the time in her bag. It looks like a finger from a fist pointing up at her, and there have been speculations as to what it was. One idea is that it is a materialised hand, with the finger pointing at the light beam to show it's significance in some way, with the bag acting as a 'cabinet' for the ectoplasm, but there is no other evidence to support that at the moment.

On another occasion, a friend asked if Jo would run a meditation circle at her home. She agreed, and they gathered at her house. She had replaced the bulb in her living room lamp, with a red one. Jo had no idea why she had done this, but she seemed happy with her preparations. Everyone started to arrive and take their seats. As one lady walked across the room accompanied by her daughter, Jo noticed she was limping. Jo enquired as to what was wrong with her leg, and she told her she had fallen a couple of weeks earlier,and that it was still swollen and difficult to put weight on properly. For some reason, Jo immediately offered to give healing. This was strange, because although she had never doubted the power of spirit to heal, she had never actually placed her hands on anyone before. Her daughter immediately started saying, Oh that's daft, all that nonsense, but the lady motioned to her daughter to be quiet, and said well yes, I would appreciate you trying.

Jo threw her thoughts to the guides, and asked for a healing to take place. As soon as she put her hands upon the knee, a dark hand, almost like a hand wearing a black glove, appeared over Jo's. She was shocked, to say the least, but completely mesmerised at the same time. This hand seemed to dart through her fingers, and inside the ladies knee. She couldn't remove her hands if she had wanted to at that point, as it seemed they were almost glued to her. Jo could feel things being moved around under her hands. She glanced at the woman, who was just sat staring in complete surprise at what was going on. Her daughter started to stutter, " I can see something, oh my God, what is going on!" All the others in the room had gathered around to watch this event take place. After a few moments, the hand seemed to withdraw from her knee, and appear over Jo's once again. Then it was gone, it vanished as quickly as it had appeared. Her hands became un-glued, and she sat back on her heels. She looked at the woman, and said um, what happened there? The woman said nothing, got to her feet, and walked, minus the limp, across the room. Her daughter at this point had stopped stuttering and was completely unable to talk.

The meditation circle did not take place that night, instead there was a long and exciting debate. Many healings have taken place under similar circumstances to that one since then.

Then there was the curious case of the apported books. Jo had ordered from a well known on-line book site, Lights and Shadows of Spiritualism, written by DD Home. It was a rare book, having been written in the late 1800's. There were two copies for sale, both in the United States. Jo ordered one, and waited for it to arrive.

It was quite strange really, because whenever she had purchased a book before, she had been unable to put it down until she'd read every page. However, when this book arrived, she flicked through the pages, and then stashed it on her shelf along with other books in her bedroom, where it stayed for several weeks.

Sometime later on a chilly night, she had a long soak in the tub, then decided to settle in bed and start to read it. She switched on her bedside lamp, pulled down the duvet, went to check the house was all locked up, entered her bedroom, took the book from the shelf, slipped into bed, turned to her bedside cabinet to get her glasses, and there staring at her on the cabinet was another copy of the book she was holding.! She looked at it in sheer amazement, and then at the book in her hand, they were both exactly the same! She was bewildered to say the least. She rang a friend the following morning to see what she made of it, but she was as bemused as Jo was.

A few days later, Jo saw her friend, who examined both copies in detail, and there was not one difference between them. Jo gave her one copy, as it was a book that she did not have either.

A few weeks later, another friend was visiting and Jo relayed the incident of the book to him. He asked if he could borrow the copy she had kept, which Jo agreed to, but several months passed and he did not return it, and to this day has still not. However, at a later date, she went to her bookcase in the dining room, and there she found yet another copy. Jo felt there must have been a message, or something she was intended to identify with, within its pages. And where had these books come from? A great mystery. Jo realised that all this would probably be impossible to believe, unless it had happened to yourself. Copies of books don't just turn up like that!

Chapter 10: Night-time disturbances

Jo has had lots of night-time disturbances, and describes two of them :

"Physical mediumship has not only been a part of my waking hours but often extends into my hours of slumber. These night time disturbances are a part of my spiritual work that, can at times cause me concern. Concern, because they come without warning and often are repeated until I gain an understanding of a situation, and concern because these occurence's are real happenings taking place in some poor souls life.This more un-nerving aspect of my work began shortly after my home circle started to sit and have continued to the present day, but I must highlight that there are long periods of time usually between these night time manifestations.I will recount two incidences here for you the enquirer, but for the well being of those involved will change their names.

'It was early autumn and the weather had become much cooler at night, as I snuggled under my warm duvet it wasn't long before I could feel myself drifting towards sleep.   I slept for a few hours before I was woken with a heavy weight pressing down either side of my body pinning the duvet tightly against me, I was startled to say the least and as I lay there struggling to free myself, the duvet began to be pulled up over my head. My heart started beating really quickly as I felt panic set in, whatever or whomever was doing this was using such force that physically I could not free myself, I started to manouver one hand upwards towards my head and managed to slip my fingers through a small gap above my head. To my horror I felt long wiry hair, I started to wrap my fingers in the hair until I had a fair amount firmly in my grip and I started to pull as hard as I could and, as I pulled I felt a sudden release of my duvet and the hair simply vanished within my grip, as quick as the manifestation had arrived so it left. I sat upright in bed switched on the light and scanned the room for any presence that may still be lurking, it had gone, well I say gone, it had gone for the rest of that night but returned a couple of days later, I found this experience somewhat traumatic and had to spend the next three nights sleeping with the lamp on, to try to prevent it from returning. It was not until a week or two later when I had gone to visit my mother in Somerset that I was introduced to a woman not previously known to me, that this manifestation belonged to, well I say belonged to, that's not right either, I should say I met the poor soul who was being plagued by this manifestation night after night, I will call her Julie for the purpose of this account. I discovered that Julie was infact a natural medium herself but was scared of her own abilities with her connection to spirit. I sat and chatted with Julie for quite a while and discovered that mentally she was not in a good space, she was like a scared rabbit caught in the headlights of a speeding car. I went through some spiritual exercises with her, but in particular how to close herself to spirit contact until she decides the time is right for her to embrace her gift, this included detaching the energy that was repeatedly terrifying her during the night. The night time manifestation had grown in strength through Julie's own fear of spirit and rather than embracing her gift she feared it and was being controlled because she had no understanding of it either.'

 The second incident that I recount to you here was equally as disturbing to me but for a very different reason.

'One night I was awoken by a scratching sound which seemed to be on the bottom of my bedroom door, I lay there trying to figure out what was causing it, after a couple of minutes the sound stopped, I relaxed believing it to be a natural cause, however a moment later I felt a very strange vibration at my feet which started to move upwards until it was completely on top of me, now I always sleep on my stomach so this energy was in actual fact on top of me behind, as I lay there absolutely bewildered with what was occurring to my horror realised this entity was infact a sexual predator or to be more precise would of been when he had been in the physical here in life. To make matters worse a very strong smell of aniseed filled my room, I was unable to move until this predator had completed his task, and when I had felt him slip back down the bed away from me, I became angry. Knowing now that these things are brought to me to alert me to the fact that someone is living through this night time horror, I acknowledged to my guides the fact that I had understood and would endeavour to find the person this experience related too, but that under no circumstances did I want or need to have the experience repeated to me again!!

A few days later I was running a psychic night at a local venue, I had a couple of other psychic's that were providing readings to those attending and my daughter was taking the bookings at the desk. She had come straight from work and had not eaten so was very hungry. Her partner arrived with a small picnic for her to munch on and amongst the goodies was a small tub of jelly beans. The partner of one of the psychic's who I will call Claire was sat with my daughter, and they were chatting happily to those that had arrived for a reading. My daughter had asked Claire if she wanted the black jelly beans as she didn't like them, they happened to be Claire's favourite. As I approached the desk where the pair of them were sat I was suddenly overwhelmed with the smell of aniseed, I asked where the smell was coming from, Claire replied they were the flavour of the jelly beans that she was eating, immediately I knew the person I was seeking was infact Claire. I asked Claire if I could speak with her privately to which she agreed and asked her directly if she was having problems during the night to which she responded that she was, and that she was being very troubled with bad dreams in which she is trying to run from someone.

I told her of my experience with the sexual predator entity and she immediately identified the person from her childhood, I asked her if she knew what the scratching sound was and she said yes, this person had kept his money under the floor boards and when he had retrieved it, he had made a scratching sound each time trying to lift the boards. I believe the smell of aniseed was brought to me by my guides as an indicator for identification purposes. Claire had been going through a period in her life when she said her feelings had tried to resurface and she was trying to block them out, which is probably why this experience had manifested at this time, we spoke at length and I gave her firm instructions as to how to deal with the problem. The following day I received positive news from her, she had an undisturbed night having carried out the instructions I had given her, so hopefully the situation has now been resolved and she will no longer be troubled by this unwanted entity again.'

These are just two of the night time disturbances I have experienced over the years, there have been a fair few, each coming out of the blue and each in their own way, as unnerving as each other, the life of a physical medium certainly brings some challenges with it!"

Chapter 11: I see for myself

The opportunity arose for me to attend my first physical mediumship workshop, organised by 'Spirit Connexions', and run by mediums Jo Bradley and Gail Peacock. It was held in a village hall near Bedford, in November 2011. I was open-minded about what might take place.

Jo set up a circle of chairs in the hall, which had a hard tiled floor. There were 14 students, who were asked to introduce themselves, and tell of any experiences if they wished to.

Jo then began her teaching talk, to explain, simply and directly, what is physical mediumship, and give some of her own experiences. She emphasised that a physical circle works on a love link, the guides work with love. Perhaps one in a 100,000 has physical mediumship ability, and even those might not choose to develop it. She went on to say that she has previously experienced choking dreams, like chewing gum, and something protruding from her mouth, in the middle of the night, which woke her. Was it ectoplasm? This is all part of the indicators of her ability of physical mediumship.

She continued that physical mediumship is objective, all must be able to see it or sense the same. Jo's different guides show themselves in numerous ways. Jo's circle sees spirit lights, or mists in the circle, which is ectoplasm. It changes from mist to swirling and develops in to forms.

Jo and sitters have been levitated in the circle, and trumpets which are regularly levitated and which are made of aluminium are used for direct voice, and on one occasion the guides tore one trumpet in half as if made from paper. This demonstrates that which we perceive as solid in our physical world can be altered in dimension and shape by those on spiritside.

Direct voice has been heard through the trumpet. Direct writing has been done on apported paper, where the spirit writes with a pen directly on the paper, without the use of the medium's hand, unlike automatic writing where the medium's physical hand is required.

Jo went on to talk about elongation, under red light conditions, where it has been seen and photographed with fingers extended to a far greater length.

They have seen partial materialisations in the circle. They sit in dim white light, a candle or red light, as it must be seen with the physical eyes.

Jo explained that trance is sometimes used to get the circle going, there are two types. One is where the medium's vocal chords are used by a communicator in spirit to speak, the other where the medium is unconscious. A physical circle needs a physical medium and at least one sitter, but ideally the circle should have four or five sitters to generate enough energy. However, harmony among the sitters is the most important ingredient, without it the circle will fail.

Transfiguration is a mask in front of the medium's face, ectoplasm is used to create the mask. There are numerous photographs showing Jo during transfiguration.

Spirit photography, which is a new sensitivity which Jo has developed recently, captures images, part or full, in photographs of those in spirit.

Table tilting is a basic form of communication but can be highly evidential. Jo and Gail use table tilting in their workshops because it usually brings much laughter as attendees chase tables being moved at high speed around the hall. Laughter is excellent at heightening vibrations and creating harmony among those present.

Jo then passed around some of her physical evidence for the students to see. It included some apported notes written by guides directly on paper, and drawings produced by her child guide in her home circle.

The dangers to mediums were explained. On one occasion, an investigator from a Fellowship attended a seance, and pulled the cabinet curtain back too early, which caused a burn blister near Jo's eyes, from the ectoplasm rushing back.

In reply to a question about unwelcome spirits coming in, Jo explained that like attracts like, jokers can come in, but her circle works by a healing connection. Jo was asked if every person was a suitable sitter, in developing a circle. Her response was, unfortunately, no. For instance, newly bereaved people are not really suitable until they have completed their grieving process. Each of us when we suffer a bereavement, particularly a loved one, become engulfed in a need to be able to re-connect with the person they have physically lost. This generally means that in circle mentally having desires for their lost one to come through. That transpires for the other sitters in the circle to also have a desire for the wish to be fulfilled. This creates a barrier which the guides find difficult to overcome and generally halts the development of the group. Those with a chronic illness are not ideal sitters in the developmental stages of a physical circle as the guides and sitters will have a strong desire to channel healing which alters the dynamics and intentions of those sitting.

The circle should start off as it wishes to continue, for example whether or not to use light, recorder, music and singing.

A circle leader needs to be in control on the physical side, as a guide is in control on the spirit side. We work as a partnership on both sides of the veil, but each of us with free will. Jo has a dedicated locked seance room. Her circle is private, only invitations from the guides can give access to visit the circle. They are trying to get full form materialisation at the moment and have no guest sitters, but partial forms are seen.

Jo says that all circles go through phases when nothing seems to be happening, but spirit is still working, trust them, and progress will come. Jo asked me to comment on my experiences as a sitter, and I remarked on experiences during sittings with Stewart Alexander and Colin Fry, and in two private physical circles.

Jo said never clap in circle, as it can disperse the energy, and don't whistle or whisper as these can be the first signs of direct voice, or the first signs might be missed. Clairvoyance should never be used, as this is counter-productive to production of objective evidence.

Jo and Gail then began a series of experiments designed to indicate paranormal powers. Firstly, Jo set up 3 tables about 2.5 feet square, with metal legs. Four or five students worked on each table, with hands or fingers touching the table. My group could not get the table moving at all, but the other two were sliding around the room. Interestingly, as soon as Jo came over to join us, it moved very well straight away right down the hall! At times the tables would balance on two legs and an end would lift up to a foot high and stay there until asked to go back. I had tried to push the table with my hands on the table top to see if it was possible, but my hands just slipped, having no grip. I asked for only fingertips on the table, but it still moved. This was all in ordinary daylight, and I videoed a few clips of the table movements. As a result of this, I was convinced that Jo had physical mediumship powers, because in the past I had proved for myself that genuine table movement and tilting required the presence of a physical medium. Without one, nothing genuine happens, in my experience.

Gail Peacock, a medium and the organiser, then provided a lovely lunch, followed by an EVP (electronic voice phenomena) experiment. Various recorders were switched on, and each of us in turn said who we were, with a short time after each to listen for EVP on the playback.

Next was psychic photography. Flashes on our cameras were disabled, because ectoplasm is light sensitive, too much light will make the ectoplasm retract back in to the medium at a rapid rate and can cause serious injury. The curtains were closed, but it was still quite light in the hall. Each student sat in a chair while the others took photos. First impressions were that one photo had two extra images looking very like faces. As students crowded round to look, I thought that one image looked like William, who is a spirit guide of Jo.

Lastly, Jo and Gail conducted a seance, but it was still quite light in the room. Trumpets and bells were placed in the circle, but nothing was moved. The students all seemed to feel effects from the sitting. Several were yawning, cold breezes were felt, and one sitter felt quite sick.

The conditions were new and possibly unfavourable, but the table movement was definitely paranormal, as I had proved for myself, and the faces on the photo very interesting.

I attended my second workshop with Jo and Gail, in the same village hall near Bedford, on the 28th April 2012. The attendees took several photos of each other in turn, with flash disabled on the cameras, in good red light. The mediums were hoping for a transfiguration experiment. On this occasion, all the photos I took looked normal, except this one of Jo Bradley, which the mediums suggested showed transfiguration taking place.

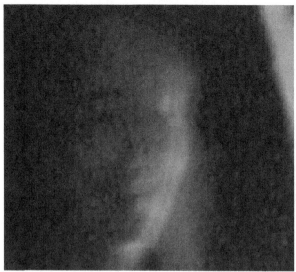

Jo Bradley transfiguration

At my third workshop, at a village hall near Basingstoke on 18th August 2012, the attendees took it in turn to sit in the cabinet in red light for a transfiguration experiment. Jo took this photo of me:

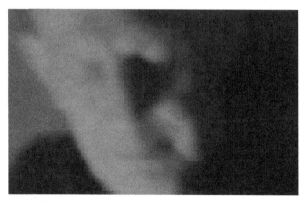

Myself, said to be transfiguring

I said my face was itching, and Jo says: "I could see the transfiguration taking place, as could the rest of the students, but we didnt realise it was to that extent!"

I had no idea there was anything over my face, although I felt itches and tingles at times. My eyes were closed throughout, and I could hear all that was said in the room, although I felt I was in a bit of a dream state. I don't know if the time of the photo corresponds, but I felt like laughing my head off and it was hard to control, then I heard the group talking about the cabinet moving. I rarely laugh my head off, it's more of a chuckle as a rule! My scientific detachment was breaking down somewhat!

In the same period as this photo was taken, other things were happening to me and the cabinet.

There was a strong red light in the cabinet, and the room was darkened with curtains but we could see each other well, as it was daytime.

As I do not consider myself mediumistic or psychic, I did not bother to get someone else to camcord me in the cabinet. I sat with closed eyes and kept very still throughout. I let myself go in to a kind of meditation with an open mind, and I could hear comments that my face was changing. I did feel some itches and tingles on my face, but I've had those before in spiritual situations. Suddenly, I heard remarks that the cabinet was moving, and it seemed that all could see this, except me of course. There was excitement in the room, and the others began to talk to the cabinet, or rather if there was a communicator causing the movement. A code was established of sideways

movement for Yes, and backwards and forwards for
No. Questions were then asked if the communicator
was male (yes), was he wanting to contact someone
here (yes), was the person to contact male (no),
female (yes). A relative (yes). Did you pass over
more than ten years ago? (yes). There were three
candidates left. Dark hair? (no) or fair hair? (yes).
The only person who was left was my fair-haired
sister, who was in attendance.

My sister accepted the communicator, but said
nothing at first. Others asked, is it a grandfather? (no).
Is it father? (no). My sister then asked, is it Ray? (
Our brother). The answer was an emphatic yes,
shown by lots of sideways swaying movement. I was
feeling very emotional by now. My sister asked, Are
you happy where you are? The answer was yes. She
was rather taken aback, and asked nothing else.
I might add that I had no sensation that the cabinet
was moving, as my eyes were closed throughout and I
was a bit dreamy, but I could hear the voices and
understand what the attendees were saying.
I confirmed the facts with the other attendees, who
said the cabinet movements were very pronounced,
and we all knew that no fraud was possible. They also
said that my face had some kind of lump on it, when
they looked at me. Although this, like table tilting, is
a basic form of communication, it proved once again
for me that the 'paranormal' is a reality, and there was
an 'intelligence' behind the answers to questions.
Beyond that, I think it's a matter of personal belief
and interpretation.

Jo Winstone, one of the attendees , says: "I can confirm everything Norman has said. It was wonderful to see his face transfiguring, and I'm so pleased the communication was for him and his sister."

The whole group of attendees with the mediums took part in table movement experiments with a large heavy table. There were some vibrations of the table, and limited movement, until Gail and most of the students left the room to prepare for the next experiment.
At this point, I asked Jo if she and I could try table movement together. Two male students came over and asked to join us. The rest of the group had left the room.
Jo asked me to lead it, and I asked, and talked to the table to please move, and it did begin to move. I became rather excited and encouraged it do more and more, shouting in fact, and it slid easily right round the room with our hands on it lightly. I asked for all four of us to remove one of our hands from the table, but it continued moving just as well. I finally asked for only one finger on it each, and the movement stopped soon after that. I have to stress that the table was large and quite heavy, and friction on the floor made it impossible to push around by hands on the top only, which I tried to do and failed.

Jo Winstone confirms what she witnessed: "I was at the workshop and can confirm Norman's account of the table tilting. When the whole group was involved with the experiment there was very little movement of the table. As soon as just Norman and Jo were joined by Paul and Robert, it took off around the room like a blooming rocket. Pretty amazing, with in the end just one finger each touching it!

Jo and Gail also run other physical mediumship courses, named ' Let's get physical!'.

One of the attendees, Caroline Tobin, was invited by Jo to her home, and to sit in the séance room with her. Caroline comments on a wonderful experience:

'Hi Jo. Thanks so much for the wonderful weekend. You so looked after me, in fact I feel like I have just left a spa! The cherry on the cake had to be when we went into your seance room, what a privilege to be part of that, and I feel so blessed to have seen a materialisation of one of your guides. I was lost for words all yesterday and have only came back to earth today! All I can say is that I was sitting in your seance room, and the next thing I saw was like a silvery cloud-like substance moving upwards from the floor. I looked away to another part of the room to make sure it wasn't my eyes adjusting to the dark, as you know I will not accept phenomena without ruling out all possibilities, but the rest of the room remained pitch black. So I looked back to the cloud-like substance and my eyes followed it upwards. Just as I was wondering what it was, I saw a face appear in that twirling cloud. It was as clear as anything. I got such a shock that I think I stopped breathing. As I continued to look, the face got clearer and clearer and a white ball of light formed around the face and was so bright it lit that end of the room. I could not believe what I was seeing and with my own physical eyes as I do not see spirit with clairvoyance. The room was so full with love that I nearly started crying. I really have been left speechless with what I saw and felt, Jo. I really feel truly blessed to have witnessed this. Truly, you and your spirit team are wonderful, and I want to thank you all for giving me the opportunity to witness my first manifestation. Thank you for being such a kind and loving soul, looking after me so well, and blowing my mind!'

Jo Bradley says: " I was right out of it, not aware of what was going on, when this took place in the séance room. I confirm that no light was on in the séance room, and Caroline told me all about this materialisation immediately afterwards."

Caroline's experience has a similarity to the materialised form in one of Jo's seances, when   Terry the circle leader was the only sitter present to witness it. They sat with a dim overhead white light, enough light so they could see each other. As mentioned before, he said it was female, seen next to Jo, and slightly behind her. It was self-illuminated and faded after a few seconds. It was like when they had seen William's head at a previous séance. The table concealed the bottom half of the figure. Terry was quite shocked at it's appearance. It seems that spirit manifestations are unpredictable and the conditions to produce them are not fully known.

Chapter 12: A rational analysis

I began to discover Jo's history of physical mediumship when I came across her website forum, in October 2009. I had been searching for the latest activity in physical mediumship, online, but was very surprised to find how much was disclosed in her site. Much evidence from their private circle, and also from spontaneous events, was freely given. There was also a circle blog, which was very unusual. In my experience, it was usually expected that an enquirer accepted the claims of mediums, without challenging or questioning the evidence, or sources, on which the claims were based. It was a matter of belief, rather than reasoned analytical conclusions from evidence. Jo's site welcomed questions, and was filled with her own evidence, which an enquirer such as me could look at rationally, besides much educational material about physical mediumship in general.

As I studied and analysed the site, I began to feel that Jo was very honest and trustworthy, and that she had complete dedication to her circle work, which had gone on twice a week for five years. I felt that it was well worth my while to really look in to the evidence, to see if it was all genuine, and as it appeared. Jo was very helpful and allowed me free access to any of her records and evidence, which was something I had always wished I might do with a medium. We developed an understanding of trust, but evidence was always very important to Jo as well as me. We had many recorded conversations about her psychic experiences, which I have included in this book.

I had already proved the paranormal for myself by sitting in physical circles, where I had experienced very active table tilting in good light, with nobody touching the table. Other minor phenomena had also occurred, and I had attended several public demonstrations given by physical mediums, but none of it had really convinced me of the reality of survival of physical death. The survival evidence given by the great mediums of the past seemed no longer available. Materialisations in light conditions were now unknown it seemed, and direct voice to me is not convincing, unless it is in a small trusted group and the validity is well demonstrated.

Gradually I pieced together Jo's story up to the point when we met online, and I asked questions which I thought were always answered with honesty by Jo. What I found was remarkable, and seemingly unique, because it all seemed to fit together like a jigsaw puzzle. I am only interested in facts and truth. The excitement mounted in myself, as I went back to the beginning and followed Jo's pathway. It appeared to be totally unique, from what I had read and experienced. Jo encouraged me to write her account in this book, and analyse it with an outsider's rational outlook.
I realised that it could still be disbelieved, as the evidence was so much at variance with what we know through orthodox science.

So I thought, could any other working model, except the Spirit one, explain all I'd learned on this project? My answer was no. There were several kinds of phenomena combined with communicator evidence which could not be accounted for by any other speculation I could think of. Occam's Razor is a well-known principle used in science and other disciplines, urging one to select from among competing hypotheses that which makes the fewest assumptions. The only competing hypothesis I could think of, to account for what I have written in this book as Jo's 'Spirit hypothesis,' is deliberate or unintentional fraud and lies by Jo and all her witnesses and contacts. There is no apparent motive for this, and would be very much more complicated to apply to the facts presented, including later some of my own experiences. The evidence in this book is both objective through physical mediumship, and subjective through mental mediumship. For the objective evidence to be false, let us see if that is reasonable.

Several members of the Circle of Friends must have lied or been mistaken about phenomena they said they witnessed. The digital photo evidence would have been faked. The hand-written notes were not apported but written and faked by Jo or others. Jo's friend and Jo's daughters made up a story and lied about the sofas moving about without them doing it, also about the furniture being moved about, objects being formed in to triangle shapes, and 23 handwritten notes, flowers, crystals, all appearing without human intervention. The models were not made by spirit Kathleen, but were made by human hands, and the circle members lied about it, or it was Jo who made the models and tricked them. The direct voices were faked and not from spirit. The ex-circle member Alec who testified when he guested at a circle gave a false statement, or Jo wrote it and passed it on to me. The direct voice at the deathbed was either a collective hallucination or the whole family lied about it.

My opinion is that it is ridiculous to accept the fraud hypothesis. Why would all the witnesses stage such a complicated fraud? Or how could they all have been so deceived about what was going on in the home and it's séance room? It was objective, and could be seen, felt, or heard.

On the other hand, a 'Spirit hypothesis' fits all the claimed phenomena as decribed in this book. Some of the phenomena could be ascribed to what scientific investigators, mostly in the 19th Century, variously termed a psychic force, or telekinesis, or psychokinesis, not involving spirits, but could equally well be caused by spirit activity in some cases. Other phenomena seems to be working towards various kinds of objective survival evidence, like direct voice from relatives already achieved, and indications of transfiguration and materialisation in lighted conditions. The trance communications back up what was produced as phenomena. My own recent involvement with Jo's workshops proved to me that, at the very least, what I experienced was paranormal, whether it was caused by a 'psychic force' or by spirit involvment. Of course, this also confirmed to me that Jo was a genuine physical medium.

When I had collected most of the data for this book, I went on a day's visit to meet Jo, and examine the evidence. By now, I could not see any way in which I had been deceived about my investigations with Jo, but I remained rational as always.

I found that Jo was just as nice and genuine as I had anticipated, as we went through the day. My main objective was to examine the physical evidence, which Jo stores so carefully.

I examined all the apported notes with writing on, about twenty in all, the first alleged apports I had held for myself. As I took each one from the sleeve in the album to look at, it was a strange feeling, that Spirit had apparently torn off a piece of notepaper at a place unknown, written on it, and transported it somehow in to Jo's home; just doing that once proves the paranormal, let alone twenty times. There were names, replies, and advice written on the notes, so there was intelligence behind them, that was clear to me. The notes were said to be warm when received, all in Jo's home. I wrote down notes about these apports, then I looked at the photo taken in the first circle meeting, thought to be of 'William.' Jo's 13 year old son Donovan joined us, and he confirmed some of what Jo had told me.

The circle log books were packed with physical phenomena descriptions from the five years of sittings, together with descriptions of conditions in the circle. It was absolutely fascinating, but I only had time to glance through.

I had of course also been fascinated to see scanned photos of the models said to be made in the séance room by spirit operators, which was something I had never heard of, it seemed perhaps unique, but here were the actual models!

The first model was a crafted boat made from folded paper, which was supplied in the séance room, and twisted paper oars to go with it, but there was also a figure in it made from bluetack which had not been supplied, therefore apparently apported. The circle members had heard it being folded, and the name Kathleen was written on a piece of paper.

The second model was a boat made from plasticine, including a person's figure in it. It was made from a new packet of plasticine which the spirit operators were said to have ripped open and moulded in to shape. The colours of the strips could be seen blending in to each other, and in to quite a complex shape of the boat and the figure. Jo said that the plastic film was rubbed together and produced light effects. It was fascinating evidence of the paranormal, if true and genuine.

The third figure was of an upright person moulded from plasticine. Jo says that her tight –fitting ring was pulled from her finger and hung on the arm of the figure.

We discussed the light beam photo, and I saw the original photo and negative. Jo showed me where it was taken, where her dining room now is. There were no light sources in the room to account for that light beam photo.

Jo then showed me a battered metal trumpet. For some reason spirit had shown their power it seemed, by banging it against the walls of the séance room until it was distorted. This was quite a rigid object.

Jo then supplied a lunch of jacket potatoes and salad ,as we were beginning to flag with the heat!
Later, I met Terry, the circle leader, and he seemed very laid-back and matter-of-fact about his circle experiences, as though it was 'normal'. My visit had not shown me any reason to doubt the evidence presented by Jo.
A believer in Spiritualism, or spirit interaction with our physical world, might interpret all that happened with an account something like this:

"Individuals in the Spirit World do try to help us on the Earth plane, and look for mediums who can help fulfil their purpose. A team of Spirits recognised that, potentially, Jo had the gifts and the dedication to work with them as a physical medium in a special way.
They inspired Tony Stockwell to encourage Jo to investigate this, and they grabbed her attention by providing instant phenomena in her seances. They wanted tangible evidence above all, and a spirit was there to be photographed as they wanted, though in the dark, and it looked like white mist to the sitters. When uploaded, the image was of a man, said to be with a beard, floating on his side. Levitation of the table happened on the first sitting as well. So there was both a photographic identity, and physical movement phenomena, to grab Jo's attention.

Just after this Spirit provided apports, more evidence against known scientific laws. The apported notes were not only what is termed paranormal, but had names written on them, indicating intelligence and identity. This was the very rare direct Spirit writing, not automatic writing, the paper came from elsewhere, and there were witnesses to the apports. This all fitted Spirit activity.

Furniture was then moved around in her house and gained her family's attention while they were just sitting there, again there is no accepted scientific explanation. But Spirit have been said to do this countless times in past times. This was backed up by triangles being formed in the home from objects, indicating again intelligence behind it. This was unmistakeable phenomena, with witnesses of it, particularly when the house was disarranged by other forces and an apported note with names on it was found, followed by apported notes with answers to questions which were stored for evidence.

The only non-Spirit cause for all these apports was fraud and deception by Jo. But no motivation was obvious, and there were many witnesses, family and friends, who saw it happen. They would all have to be in on any deception as well.

Spirit are said to try to use what channels of communication they can, and in the case of the Lucy EVP and the accurate prophecy about the future poltergeist case Jo dealt with, this fits the facts of what happened. A purely coincidental chain of events as recorded is very hard to believe, if fraud is ruled out.

As would be expected the group was developed and began to get the beginnings of direct voice and materialising, which fits the model from past experiences of mediums.

The trance reading with Jay Love, who did not know Jo, and could have been anybody, backed up her personal contact with Spirit by saying she had knowledge to produce physical mediumship, and was wanted to work that way for Spirit. We are told that physical mediums are very rare perhaps one in a hundred thousand of the population. So was this a lucky guess? Well, there was a large amount of prophecy in two further trance readings, with Paul Case this time, and very firmly placing her in a very special physical mediumship role. To have three readings all highlighting this seems quite convincing, that guides were indeed aware of what she was doing, and linking up through the trance mediums.

Further development in the circle showed that the Spirit model was still working, and contact with deceased family members began to happen by direct voice and other methods. This is ongoing, and there is nothing which prevents the Spirit interpretation of what has happened to Jo, family and circle being the correct one."

Each reader must make up his or her mind about how to interpret what is described in this book. As a scientist, I found much of it very hard to believe, because it appeared to contradict the known scientific laws of Nature. But then, science is continually learning more, and adapting it's theories, so who knows what new laws will one day be discovered, to account for these kinds of experiences?

This book is dedicated to truth. Should you wish to contact me or Jo with any questions, our email addresses are: normanhutt@btinternet.com or jo.bradleycircle@talktalk.net

<u>Photo Appendix from Jo Bradley mediumship</u>

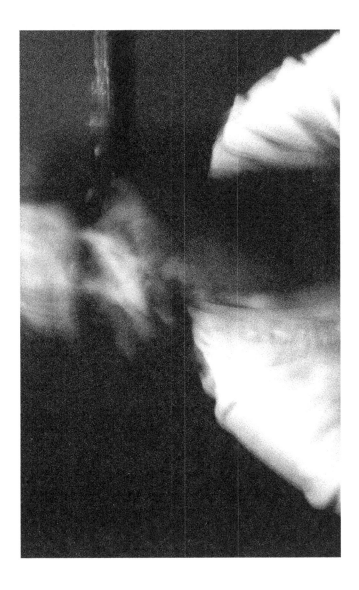

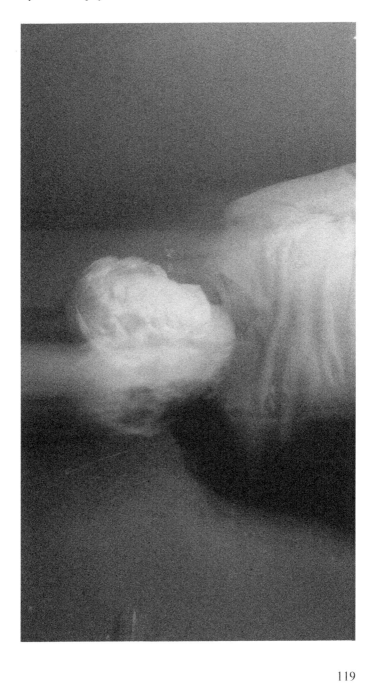

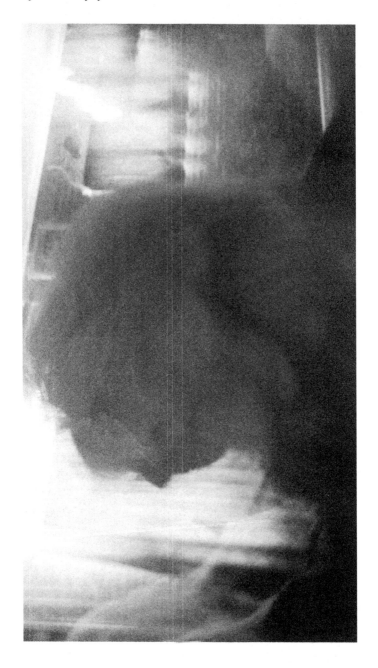

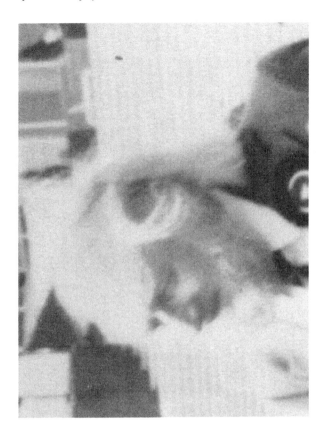

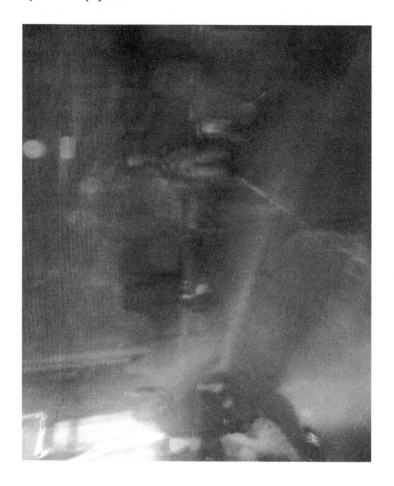

Spirit in the physical

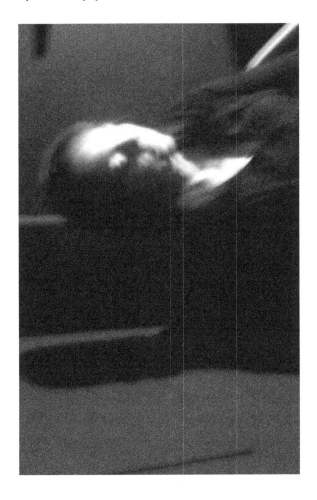

Spirit in the physical

Spirit in the physical

Spirit in the physical

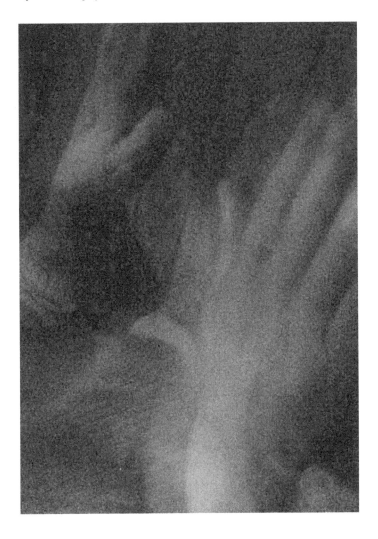

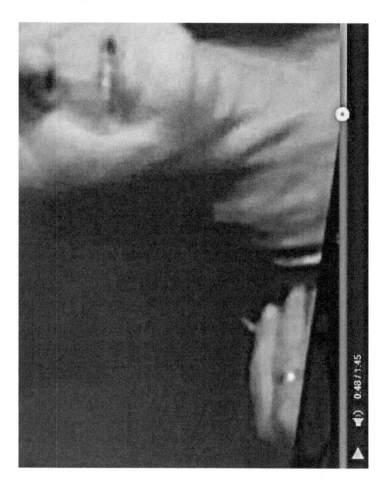

Spirit in the physical

Spirit in the physical

Spirit in the physical

Spirit in the physical